T0311620

Towards a Critique of Architecture's Contemporaneity

Pursuing historical analogies between nineteenth-century theories and the current practices captivated by digital reproducibility, this book offers a critical take on architecture's contemporaneity through four essays: tectonics, materiality, cladding, and labor. Fundamental to this proposition is the historicity of Gottfried Semper's theorization of architecture amidst the outpouring of new materials and construction techniques during the 1850s. Starting with Semper's differentiation between theatricalization and the tectonic of theatricality, this book examines thematic essential to architecture's self-representation. Even though the title of this book recalls the Semperian Four Elements of Architecture, its argument encapsulates a unique historico-theoretical project probing the tectonic of theatricality beyond Semper. The invisible tie between technique and labor is the cord running through the four subjects covered in this book. In exploring these subjects from the theoretical standpoint of Marxian dialectics, this book's contribution is focused on, but not limited to, the topicality of labor today when its relationship with capital has been further obscured by the prevailing digitalization of commodity exchange value, starting roughly in the 1990s. Each essay examines Semper's theorization of architecture in contradistinction to the ways in which technology's mediation has dominated architecture's representation.

Burrowing through the invisible tie between technique and work, asymptomatic of architecture's predicament in global capitalism, *Towards a Critique of Architecture's Contemporaneity* advances the scope of architectural criticism beyond the exhausted formalism and architecture's turn to philosophy circa the 1980s and the present tendencies for presentism. It will therefore be of interest to researchers and students of architectural history and theory.

Gevork Hartoonian is a Professor Emeritus at the University of Canberra, Australia, and holds a Ph.D. from the University of Pennsylvania, USA.

He has taught in American universities, including Pratt Institute and Columbia University, NYC. He has been a visiting professor of architectural history at Tongji University, Shanghai, in 2013 and 2016. During these visits, he also delivered lectures at the South East University, Nanjing, and the China Academy of Arts, Hangzhou. Hartoonian is most recently the author of *Reading Kenneth Frampton: A Commentary on Modern Architecture 1980* (2022) and *Time, History and Architecture: Essays on Critical Historiography* (2018). His previous publications include, among others, *Global Perspectives on Critical Architecture* (2015), *The Mental Life of the Architectural Historian* (2013), and *Architecture and Spectacle: A Critique,* (2012). The Korean and Thai editions of his *Ontology of Construction* (1994) were published in 2010 and 2017. Hartoonian is currently editing a book entitled *The Visibility of Modernization in Architecture: A Debate* (Routledge, forthcoming).

Towards a Critique of Architecture's Contemporaneity

4 Essays

Gevork Hartoonian

Routledge
Taylor & Francis Group

LONDON AND NEW YORK

First published 2023
by Routledge
4 Park Square, Milton Park, Abingdon, Oxon OX14 4RN

and by Routledge
605 Third Avenue, New York, NY 10158

Routledge is an imprint of the Taylor & Francis Group, an informa business

© 2023 Gevork Hartoonian

British Library Cataloguing-in-Publication Data
A catalogue record for this book is available from the British Library

Library of Congress Cataloging-in-Publication Data
Names: Hartoonian, Gevork, author.
Title: Towards a critique of architecture's contemporaneity: 4 essays /
Gevork Hartoonian.
Description: Abingdon, Oxon: Routledge, 2023. |
Includes bibliographical references and index. |
Identifiers: LCCN 2022050849 (print) | LCCN 2022050850 (ebook) |
ISBN 9781032418681 (hardback) | ISBN 9781032419329 (paperback) |
ISBN 9781003360445 (ebook)
Subjects: LCSH: Architecture–Philosophy. | Labor.
Classification: LCC NA2500 .H378 2023 (print) | LCC NA2500 (ebook) |
DDC 720.1–dc23/eng/20221026
LC record available at https://lccn.loc.gov/2022050849
LC ebook record available at https://lccn.loc.gov/2022050850

ISBN: 978-1-032-41868-1 (hbk)
ISBN: 978-1-032-41932-9 (pbk)
ISBN: 978-1-003-36044-5 (ebk)

DOI: 10.4324/9781003360445

Typeset in Baskerville
by KnowledgeWorks Global Ltd.

Contents

Introduction

I want to start this introduction with a world re-known architectural photographer, Nelson Kon's recollection of the event of taking pictures of Alvaro Siza's Camargo Museum, Brazil. Similar to other cultural spectacles of late capitalism, he and another three photographers were doing their best to choose the best of the best light, angle, and "best framing for a picture worthy of the narcissism of that body-object, able to catch the eye of publishers and readers alike, eager for novelty and visual excitement."[1] If we zoom out of the stage Kon set, we get a larger picture of the state of global reproduction and consumption of cultural products. The body-object axiom is inseparable from humanity's evolutionary process to the point that seeing, touching, selecting, and getting excited about the work was taken for granted until the emergence of the age of mechanical reproducibility. To follow the stage set above and following Walter Benjamin, it is convincing to say that the modernist appropriation of art and architecture began with the invention of photography and film even though machines and industrially made tools were already mediating between the hand and the object at both production and consumption processes.[2] The claim is that in different ways, film and photography armed humanity to reproduce "images" with particular effects and affects beyond the image an artist or an architect had in mind. What made this unfolding Historical was its coincidence with the Marxian formulation of the fetishism of commodities, foreshadowing a specter that since then has overridden the use-value and labor essential to producing any commodity, including architecture. For Fredric Jameson, the labor's specter is the "back-breaking millennial toil of millions of people from the earliest moment of human history,"[3] from women's work as the oldest division of labor to the ones enforced by digital reproducibility. Arantes Pedro Fiori writes that in the frozen image

DOI: 10.4324/9781003360445-1

of the photographer's objective lens, "the work appears to be a fetish of itself with its clean and untouched surface, not yet eroded by the passage of time and people. The image replaced, with certain advantages, the object itself." The age of digital reproducibility has elevated image-building as a cultural phenomenon, if not a pandemic disease, thanks to the intensity of contemporary time and space experience in late capitalism, even though Jameson pushes the time-space antinomy to its extreme, claiming that "in the postmodern time has become space anyhow."[4]

In this book, I advance the following thesis: that Gottfried Semper's differentiation between theatricalization and the tectonic of theatricality is essential to critique the contemporaneity of architecture. The ideas presented in the compiled four essays are fundamental to this proposition, each of which probes one aspect of Semper's formulation of the tectonic of theatricality. Of the four interrelated topics covered—tectonics, materiality, cladding, and labor, the latter is the most critical; it addresses issues that Semper did not discuss explicitly, even though labor had attained visibility in everyday life of mid-nineteenth-century England and the romantic discourses promoted by the prominent members of the Arts and Crafts movement. Probing the subject from the theoretical standpoint of Marxian dialectics, the argument underlines the topicality of labor today, even when its relation with capital has been obscured by the prevailing digitalization of commodity exchange value since the second digital turn roughly in the 1990s.

Two analogical similitudes inform this book's historico-theoretical assumption. Firstly, the coincident of major technological transformation that relates to and keeps apart the present digital age from nineteenth-century mechanical reproducibility. Modernization is the central magnet of these two ages, which has attained a global scale during the last two decades, and its significant aspects were already on show in the famous Great Exhibition, London, 1851. Not only that, the central figure of this narrative actively witnessed and participated in the phantasmagoria displayed in the Crystal Palace; like most historically self-conscious architects and thinkers, Semper could not but re-think architectural theory anew. This last point is, in fact, the second analogical similitude that informs the discussion presented in each chapter of this book. Semper's theorization of architecture was unique then and useful today if read along with a Derridian deconstruction strategy and beyond historicism that would box him along the Foucauldian discursive formations of the time, at best. Even though he felt obliged to tally with the language of Renaissance architecture, Semper's theorization of architecture drew from essential building elements, enough reason to consider his proposed four elements an alternative to the universalism attributed to classical Orders. I want to go further and suggest that Semper's tectonics should be construed as the four poles of the semiotic rectangle. Thus, on one pole, we have the art-form, core-form, and on the other, the earth-work framework plotted in binary opposition. In passing, I should say that the relationship between these four poles is not deterministic but diachronic; a change in one pole might initiate changes in others depending on their intrinsic potentialities. Without penning as such, this reading was central to my first encounter with Semper's radical agenda.[5]

Tectonics is a complex idea and should not be reduced to a recipe for practice but appropriated as a critical tool for historical criticism, even though the scale of architecture has surpassed what was proper to Semper's tectonics in contradistinction to then the large-scale work of engineering.[6] The suggested four poles embrace various materials and skills available in each turn of the technological apparatus of a given time and place without disclaiming Semper's association of each with the ur-form of his proposed four industries; masonry, carpentry, ceramics, and textiles. Not only the term industry as such was not uttered in pre-nineteenth-century architectural treatises, but Semper's deconstructing origins of architecture were also hypothesized in almost every treatise since Vitruvius's *De architectura* (20 BCE), later published as *The Ten Books on Architecture*. In *Der Stil* (the 1860s), Semper plots a historical and technical constellation, emptying the building art's elements from historicism.[7] The Semperian four elements should be read as a matter of fact without necessarily needing textual theorization, as is also the case with the digital, even though architects would theorize both. Suppose the reader agrees with my proposition that since the second turn to digital, the hot days of architectural theories practiced during the 1980s have been frozen. In that case, we have another reason for Semper's relevance today.

Highlighting the symbolic language of Renaissance architecture, what makes Semper appealing today is his analytical approach to promoting a single mandate: that the dialogical rapport between surface articulation and the masonry constructed form should be attended anew, given his distrust of iron's suitability for civic architecture. The first chapter traces the profound relationship between nineteenth-century theories and the present digital architecture through the lens of the changing concept of historicity. I pursue this historico-theoretical project in a discussion that focuses on the column and the wall and the impact of contemporary technification on architecture. It intends to highlight the genesis of Semper's notion of *excess* in architecture, the tectonic of theatricality.

Central to the transformation from mechanical to digital reproducibility is matter and its change into materiality. The architectonic of which, along with invested labor, is evaporated in the ever-increasing intrusion of commodity form into the culture of the building, from design to the production of mass customized and animated surfaces. The haptic and tactile dimensions of the material discussed in the second chapter are essential to the differentiation of cladding and materiality. The actuality of technic dis-proportionally undervalued in the empathic technological impact on human sense perception, that is, the hardness, softness, and lightness of a work. The fluidity of contemporary surface architecture is measured in the intensity of time-space, and the mobility digitalization has instigated most facets of everyday life. The chapter argues that the dialectics between materiality and appearance is essential to architecture, even though its mode of operation and appropriation has varied throughout architectural history. The historicity of contemporary architecture and the importance of material and its transformation into materiality are pursued at two historical moments, the Renaissance and early modernism. Particular attention is given to the writing of Leon Battista Alberti, John Ruskin, and Adolf Loos, respectively.

In the state of contemporary digitalization of architecture, the idea of surface, the Semperian dressing, has emerged as formative for digital architecture. Taking advantage of the Dom-ino structural system, architecture today showcases its surface beyond any representational restrain, including the Corbusian free-façade and the symbolism of Renaissance architecture. Paradoxically, Renaissance is the classical edition of the free-façade anchored to the masonry enclosure. Mapping the differences between dressing and dressed-up, the third chapter outlines Semper's reluctance to fully engage with the impact of building industrialization and the expressive dimension of emerging industrial materials. Semper's concern with the non-malleability of iron for civic architecture echoed in the Miesian steel and glass tectonics and the notion of "thickening the wall," evident in the late work of Le Corbusier and Louis I. Kahn. Thus the relevance of the clothing (covering) for contemporary architecture and for exploring the historical coincidence between the impact on the architecture of the technological transformations unfolding today and during the late nineteenth century. Central to this observation is the phenomenal material change into materiality essential to understanding architecture's uneven dialogue with time.

The fourth chapter focuses on the complex rapport between architecture and temporality in conjunction with two Marxian prejudices: that temporality is not a choice but an attribute of a particular stage of the commodity production system. And that a critical analysis of temporality and labor necessitates an historico-theoretical project that should depart from the present state of architectural praxis. I argue that the acceleration of temporality evident in parametric design and the variety of reproduced forms is an aspect of the capitalistic project to extinguish the past of labor at the expense of accommodating and disseminating the commodity form across cultural products, architecture included. The chapter focuses on how the spectral nature of the aesthetic of commodity fetishism has been heightened at the expense of detail.

In each chapter, I examine Semper's theorization of architecture in contradistinction to technology's mediating role then and now. Approaching the four themes as symptoms of architecture's entanglement with global capitalism, this book advances a critique of the contemporaneity of architecture beyond the already exhausted formalism and architecture's turn to philosophy circa the 1980s. I read Semper through the available literature on his writings and in the light of Benjamin's seminal essay, "The Work of Art in the Age of Mechanical Reproducibility," and Jameson's Marxian critique of the logic of contemporary culture, wherein the technological dictates a new style while "responding more adequately to the aims of the investments,"[8] and it's multivalent bearings on material, skill, and labor. Benjamin highlights the importance of the immediacy of the present for a Marxian understanding of the past of the distance though infused with *time-now*. This project traces the profound relationship between nineteenth-century theories and the present digital architecture through the lens of the changing concept of historicity. I pursue this historico-theoretical project in a discussion focusing on Semper's theorization of tectonic theatricality. In addition to the re-surfacing of the *surface* in digitally reproduced architecture, I posit this unfolding, a theme central to Semper's theorization of the principle of dressing and the tectonics, the untold story of why Semper has become topical today.

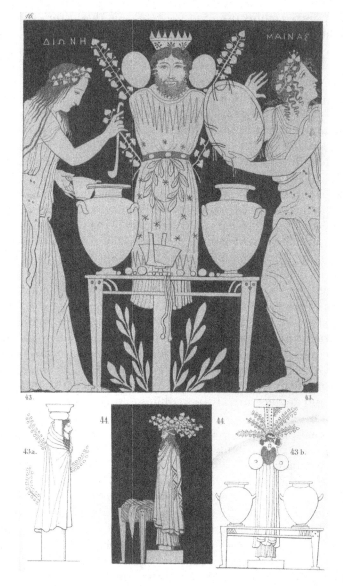

Figure 0.1 Baum Bekleidung, "tree dressing," in Carl Bötticher, Der Baumklutus Der Hellenen, Berlin, 1856.

Source: Image courtesy of Spyros Papapetros.

I want to end this introductory remark by sharing another spectacular event though an ancient one, the story of Apollo chasing Daphne.[9] It is the tale of the metamorphosis of a young woman into a tree while being tracked. There are three issues relating Daphne to the subject; the tectonic theatricality explored in this book's each chapter to the point that the reader will not dismiss overlapping issues from one to the next chapter. Here and there, I also take advantage of my previous writings on Semper throughout the book, especially on the difference between theatrical tectonics and theatricalization and the exhibitionist quality of digital architecture. This is important because both ideas enjoy a degree of animation, the first issue relating to Daphne's story. The second is the notion of metamorphosis, the transformation of a building into architecture, from core-form to the art-form, a schism dismissed by a straight-jacket modernist, form follows function, and the postmodernist simulacra. Like Jacques Lacan's reading of Daphne, Semper's tectonic of theatricality "challenges presuppositions regarding the functionalist origins of architecture," writes Spyros Papapetros.[10] More related to the argument presented in the following pages is Carl Bötticher's description of "tree dressing," as part of Greece tradition (Figure 0.1). A vertical wooden shaft dressed up with clothes and laurels, looking part human and part natural (tree), a sacrificial ornament perhaps in anticipation of Alberti's proclamation of the column as ornament par excellence, discussed in chapter 1. Bötticher did not support the idea of the wooden hut as the origin of architecture; however, the reference to the mythic "tree dressing" was analogous to the distinction he made between the core-form and art-form Semper borrowed to formulate the tectonic theatricality.

Today, like a commodity, the animated and digitally reproduced surfaces parade and occupy every aspect of contemporary everyday life. Capitalism has successfully created a virtual enclosure, the totality of a commodified culture, and the following pages are an attempt to provide the thematic of historical criticism of architecture's contemporaneity.

Notes

1 Arantes Pedro Fiori, *The Rent of Form: Architecture and Labor in the Digital Age* (Minneapolis: The University of Minnesota Press, 2019), 5.
2 Walter Benjamin, "The Little History of Photography," Benjamin, ed. *Selected Writings Volume 2, 1927–1934* (Cambridge: Harvard University Press, 1999), 507–530.

For the notion of image and theatricality, see Michael Fried, *Why Photography Matters as Art as Never Before* (New Haven: Yale University Press, 2008).

3 To get a full picture of the essentiality of labor in History, see Jameson "Marxism and Historicism," in Jameson, ed. *The Ideologies of Theory* (London: Verso, 2008), especially 464–468.

4 Fredric Jameson, "The Antinomies of Postmodernity," in Jameson, ed. *The Cultural Turn: Selected Writings on the Postmodern, 1983–1998* (London: Verso Books, 1998), 62.

5 Gevork Hartoonian, *Ontology of Construction: On Nihilism of Technology in Theories of Modern Architecture* (Cambridge: Cambridge University Press, 1994). And Kenneth Frampton, *Studies in Tectonic Culture: The Poetics of Construction in Nineteenth and Twentieth Century Architecture* (Cambridge: The MIT Press, 2001).

6 See "From Tectonic to Ornament: Towards a Different Materiality," in Antoine Picon, ed. *Digital Culture in Architecture* (Basel: Birkhauser, 2010), 115–170.

7 For a fresh take on the origin of architecture and globalization of commerce, and the discursive space Gottfried Semper experienced, see Michael Gnehm and Sonja Hiderband, *Architectural History and Globalized Knowledge: Gottfried Semper in London* (Madrid: Mendrisio Academy Press, 2022).

8 Fredric Jameson, "The Brick and the Balloon: Architecture, Idealism and Land Speculation," in *The Cultural Turn: Selected Writings on the Postmodern, 1983–1998* (London: Verso Books, 1998), 164.

9 For a full account of Daphne's contribution to arts, see Spyros Papapetros, "Daphne's Legacy," *On the Animation of the Inorganic: Art and Architecture and the Extension of Life* (Chicago: University of Chicago Press, 2012), 263–317.

10 Spyros Papapetros, *"Daphne's Legacy,"* 2012, 272.

1 On Tectonics

Starting with the *Ontology of Construction* (1993), I have written frequently on tectonics to the point that it might be almost impossible on this occasion not to reiterate parts of my previous thought on the subject. As a student of architecture in Iran, it was amusing to think of the role of frame structure in the design process. Do architects prioritize the columnar spacing of a structural system over the spatial requirements? Or does the structural system come into the picture after laying out the required spaces dictated by the brief? These queries attained a new dimension with my final graduation studio project, in which, in the spirit of Archigram and the mega-structures of the Japanese Metabolist movement, the design comprised a gigantic space-frame structure holding together both public and capsule-like residential units cast out of plastic and hung from a space-frame module! After graduation, I wished to pursue the relationship between technology and architecture at the University of Pennsylvania and to take advantage of the work and teaching of Louis I. Kahn and Robert Le Ricolais, both of whom had unfortunately passed when I landed in Philadelphia in mid-1976.

During the late 1970s, "technology" was a hot subject, as it is today. This was partly because of the International Style architecture crisis of the time and the turn to philosophical discourses; phenomenology and semiology, the two front-runners in the intellectual milieu of East Coast America. Technology had also attained visibility because of the void left by colonialism in non-Euro-American regions of the world. The emerging third-world nations, with little choice, had to accommodate the objective and subjective implications of capitalistic modernization in full bloom. Juggling with the writings of Theodor Adorno and Manfredo Tafuri on the one hand, and a host of publications on technology, including "do-it-yourself" and Mao's theory of "two steps forward, one step backward," on the other, Martin

DOI: 10.4324/9781003360445-2

Heidegger's discourses on technology and dwelling seemed promising at the time. Still, as I searched for historical analysis and understanding of why most architects were fascinated with Le Corbusier and Mies van der Rohe's architecture, three openings on the subject of construction and design seemed promising at the University of Pennsylvania at that time: Marco Frascari's interest in Carlo Lodoli and his interpretation of the poetry of making and detailing; Joseph Rykwert's writing on Leon Battista Alberti, and the analogical rapport between the body and the corporeality of the building; and Peter McCleary's course on technology, with an emphasis on Heidegger and Marx. Frascari suggested that the expressiveness of construction was suppressed by disregarding of the framework, masking the joints, and eliminating detailing.[1] The ultimate breakthrough concerning the dialectics between construction and construing occurred after reading Harry-Francis Mallgrave's dissertation, later published in a book entitled *Gottfried Semper: The Architect of the Nineteenth Century* (1996).

Along with the above autobiographical notes, as an academic with a Marxian tendency, I was uplifted by Semper's London lecture of 1851, "The Four Elements of Architecture"[2] (alluded to in the subtitle of this book). Duncan Berry's two-volume dissertation on Semper, which Mallgrave brought to my attention, was encouraging despite not having the opportunity to meet either author in person today! On the other hand, a close reading of Walter Benjamin's work offered insight into the importance of the immediacy of the *present* for a historical materialist understanding of the past, that the present has a thick skin not in phenomenological but in Benjaminian terms. In a note from the convolutes of *The Arcades Project*, Benjamin wrote, "What distinguishes images from the 'essence' of phenomenology is their historical index." He continued, "For the historical index of the images not only says that they belong to a particular time; it says above all that they attain legibility only at the particular time."[3] In other words, the present holds on to simultaneous temporalities, the collision of nameless temporalities, waiting for an unexpected occurrence to exceed historical expectations and to spill over "when history and memory are involuntarily thrown together and their differences blurred and diminished."[4] Following Benjamin's notion of "dialectical image," it's not farfetched to say that the mechanical reproducibility Semper witnessed in the construction processes of the Crystal Palace in London (1851), the coming together of the historical and event, facilitated the bursting out of "authentic historical time." Analogically, Semper's theorization of tectonics, as discussed on many occasions in this book, spilled over architecture's past and present, deconstructing the classical wisdom of the Orders. It also radicalized the debate on style, a nineteenth-century obsession. This much is evident from Semper's unbuilt project for a museum in South Kensington, London, 1855, a hybrid image combining a traditional stone base enclosure with an iron and glass transparent roof, alluding to the emerging industrial culture (Figure 1.1).[5]

Central to these preliminary observations is the triple crisis advanced in this chapter. Semper wrote the "Four Elements of Architecture" in the middle of the crisis induced by the industrial revolution. In light of breakthroughs caused by digital technology, it is relevant to explore Semper's ideas concerning the contemporary crisis of architectural praxis. At the heart of this claim is the issue of technology and its dissemination beyond the technical realm, which occurred against the backdrop of the takeover of the project of modernity by capitalism in the aftermath of World War II.[6] Tafuri has discussed this issue at a general level; for him, architecture in modernity can't but navigate from one crisis to another, and, in contrast to the nineteenth-century romanticists, he saw no way out of architecture's stalemate within the production and consumption

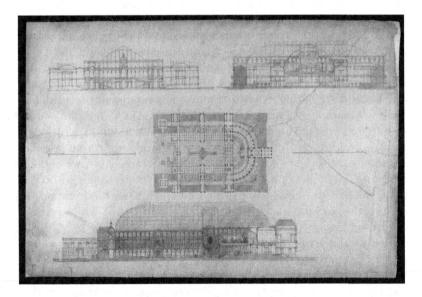

Figure 1.1 Gottfried Semper, an unbuilt project for a museum in South Kensington, London, 1855.

Source: Image courtesy of the Royal Commission for the Exhibition of 1851 archive.

system of capitalism. What had not attained full visibility at the time of Tafuri's writing was the infusion of technology into the cultural domain, including the aesthetics of architecture. Accordingly, the dissemination of theatricalization and animation across the cultural realm during the last two decades has been transformative to the point that the aesthetic of commodity fetishism is conceived and appropriated today like the Humanist appropriation of the many facets of the body-architecture analogy. Conclusive for the exploration of Semper, as presented throughout this volume, is the significance and relevance of the nineteenth century for constructive criticism of architecture's contemporaneity.

Since the 1990s' turn to digital reproducibility, the idea of tectonics has been surging. From Bernard Cache's "Digital Semper" (2000) to "tectonic imagination," a conversation between Azadeh O. Sawyer and Nader Tehrani (April 7, 2021),[7] however, these two far apart events were foreshadowed by several earlier publications, among which Kenneth Frampton's book on the subject stands tall.[8] The compilation of the best theorizations of the tectonics available today in "Reader" format should be unpacked,[9] in addition to the most recent take on Semper that plots the German architect's theory of tectonics along certain lines, similar to what the reader might take away from the following pages.[10] In analogy to the over-production of a product in the capitalistic market economy, the surge in tectonics in the context of parametric architecture has problematized the crossroad between architecture and engineering, a topic central to nineteenth-century theorizations of tectonics. During the past several decades, scientific experimentation has expanded the available generic knowledge of materials, and this, coupled with digital innovations, has enabled architects and engineers to design structures on a part with nineteenth-century engineering work and surpassing the early modernist avant-garde dream world. Strategically, we should take this opening as productive; it qualifies the tectonics with criticism needed to deconstruct the contemporary aestheticization of architecture beyond its usefulness for architects who wish to pursue critical praxis.

Two of the triple crises introduced earlier relate to the emergence of the frame structural system, and the tectonic dissociation between the column and the wall central to classical architectonics. The third, call it the crisis of *fabrication*, is consequential for the emergence of the concept of objectivity discussed elsewhere[11] and extensively elaborated by Alina Payne.[12] Starting with the third crisis, the following pages will focus on the crisis of the column and wall and the technification of architecture. The inevitable entanglement of architecture with the techniques disseminated by capitalism has transformed the art of building from a symbolic to an object-oriented product for aesthetic consumption, promoting what Benjamin discussed as the touristic appropriation of architecture. The critical importance of this transformation demands reversing Marx and Engels's formulation of the rise of the working-class consciousness from "in-itself" to "for-itself" rather than the other way around. Such a reversal is analogous to the demise of the project of the historical avant-garde and architecture's drive for autonomy at the expense of discarding the radical potentialities of any attempt to reintegrate art with life.

Crisis of Fabrication

The crisis of fabrication has a specific connotation for architecture. However, starting with the technological breakthroughs of the nineteenth century, its implications have been vaster. Such was the case with the opening of the Great Exhibition of London (1851), an essential checkpoint for most architectural historians to elucidate the impact of vicissitudes of modernization on aesthetics and construction techniques. John Paxton's design fitted the category of neither "building" nor architecture to follow Nikolaus Pevsner's distinction between the two. On the other hand, Frampton suggests that "The Crystal Palace was not so much a particular form as it was a building process made manifest as a total system, from its initial inception, fabrication, and trans-shipment, to its final erection and dismantling."[13] The Crystal Palace was an analog for the rising industrial production system, anticipating the end of the ruin and its logical ties with the classical notion of monumentality.[14] Yet, the trees planted and the fabrics hung here and there inside were to domesticate the structure's unprecedented interior space, its complete exposure to the outside world (Figure 1.2). Another novelty of its interior was to set a stage for machines and pre-modern objects as if they belonged to the same universe. It was not the classical universe but the one that, without hesitation, used old objects to inaugurate the new modern era. No wonder then that the rising new age bells, the "international" that became the emblem of the modern movement architecture and the working-class movement's unity slogan. The displayed small and large objects and the crowd rambling through recharged the crowd's subjectivity with the aesthetic of commodity fetishism. The implied "dialectics of seeing"[15] contributed to writing the introductory

Figure 1.2 Crystal Palace, London's Great Exhibition, 1851 (interior view).

Source: From Dickenson's comprehensive Pictures of the Great Exhibition, London, 1851.

chapter of the rise of the new civilization, certain aspects of which Benjamin later indexed in his magnum opus work, *The Arcades Project.*

Central to Benjamin's exposition was re-imaging the past with new techniques and materials, such as iron, used to make various objects in addition to its initial use in rails. Writing to Gershom Scholem, Benjamin conceded that nowhere was "the retrospective impulse more evident than in the forms taken by the new technologies themselves, which imitated precisely the old forms they were destined to overcome."[16] If the early photography mimicked painting, the same impulse led the early automobile to look like a carriage. Benjamin's notion of "wish-images" offers the key to the historicity of the nineteenth-century European cosmopolitan centers, a fertile land for the return of the old in the guise of the new. Benjamin wrote that like a flash of light, the sudden emergence of wish-images dialectically announces the end of a phenomenon. According to Susan Buck-Morss, the intermingling of the old with the new was symptomatic of "the collective attempts to transcend as well as illuminate the incompleteness of the social order of production."[17] These observations offer a dialectical understanding of historical time with significant connotations for understanding the contemporary situation. One should agree with Alina Payne that the Great Exhibition was the messenger of what to expect from the future. She writes, "the exhibition environment in which these objects were presented, how objects might be framed and processed (be it in museum vitrines or photographic atlases, etc.) became an urgent cultural and political act." Semper's commentary on these issues Payne continues, "decisively marked the thinking about architecture for subsequent generations, ..."[18] Apropos, the proposition that the termination of the classical perception of objectivity during the late nineteenth century and the return of the organic in contemporary digitally reproduced architecture are axiomatic to the incompleteness of the project of modernity, to recall Jürgen Habermas.[19]

Among numerous old and new objects displayed in the Crystal Palace, we should give attention to two, a fountain and the Caribbean hut. Like most nineteenth-century objects, the displayed fountain emulated the symbolic dimension of pre-modern times wherein purpose, ornament, and aesthetics were integral to an object's meaningfulness. Along with trees and draperies, the fountain displayed in the Crystal Palace sought to sustain the romanticist ethos of the time. Made in iron and sitting above a small base, the fountain had two notable features (Figure 1.3); a support footing that holds up a basin with the stand-up figure of a youth holding a fish. The iron is masked by various mondain natural elements, different leaves, and a fish in the form of a table's leg. The reused natural motives are charged with symbolic reference: the nude figure standing in the basin is perhaps an unconscious reference to "the Birth of Venus," Sandro Botticelli's painting of the 1480s. Semper might have had this and several other fountains in the Exhibition of 1851 in mind when he highlighted the importance of expressions such as Tritons, Nereids, and Nymphs in the design of a fountain even if produced for the market.[20]

The Caribbean hut differed from the examples of fountains displayed in the Great Exhibition of London (Figure 1.4). Strategically, the choice to display old objects next to the most advanced industrially produced ones was made to encourage the industrially under-developed nations to see the path to the future while at the same time highlighting the superiority of the European countries, thanks to new techniques of reproducibility. These complementary ideologies attained historical significance in Semper's analytical explanation of the Caribbean hut as presented in his London Lecture of 1853. Reading his lecture backward, we could say that "The Four Elements of Architecture" was a feat in archeology seen through the dust of time and the light emanating from the Crystal Palace, a translucent

Figure 1.3 Fountain of iron, from Catalogue of the Crystal Palace Exposition,
      London, 1851.

object in the garden! This observation solidifies Semper's deconstruction of the established mythologies of architecture's origin, most often
attributed to various images of the hut as a model. Semper's text also
entails a non-architectural theory of architecture, meaning that *architecture* evolves out of a patchwork (montage) of motifs with no architectonic history. Paying attention to the historical importance of various
branches of applied arts, Semper convincingly claims that the "history
of architecture begins with the history of practical arts." He further

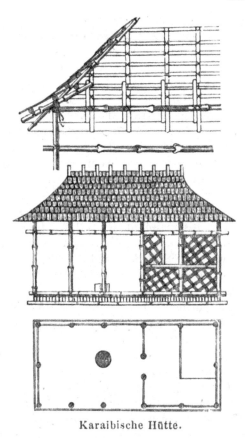

Karaibische Hütte.

Figure 1.4 Caribbean hut, Gottfried Semper, Der Stil, 1860.

Source: Image courtesy of Getty Research Institute, Los Angeles.

suggests that the molding used in architectural forms "were partly invented and practiced a long time before the foundation of architecture as a self-existing art." Thus, Semper's distinction between the art-form and the core-form was to sustain the representational dimension of architecture (the art-form) even though mechanical reproducibility had already transformed the core-form, the constructed form. Whereas this schism has been the core content of the distinction I have made between the tectonic of theatricality and theatricalization, here, and briefly, I want to expand and add another dimension to the relevance of Semper for contemporary architecture. If we agree that the global circulation of the *appearance* of commodities today adds many layers to the use value, the work of labor, is not it convincing to say that we should think of Semper's theorization of the tectonic anew? Even though the conceived duality between the art-form and the core-form was to sustain the Humanist culture of representation, from a retrospective view of history, the art-form's autonomy was a symptom of "the objective appearance" of capitalism, the appearance of "an immense collection of commodities ..., the ideological illusion of daily life,"[21] celebrated by the inauguration of the Crystal Palace.

As we will see below, the motifs Semper sought were essential for a meaningful understanding of how architectonic motifs had evolved in four industries in their most archaic developmental stage. These industries are carpentry, ceramics, textiles, and masonry. However, his claim makes it hard to imagine under what circumstances the labor and skills proper to the art-form of architecture were developed. Paradoxically, the fact that the borrowed motifs had no role in the erection of a building (the core-form) suggests that the Geist of masonry construction was already at hand, waiting to be cladded by the received motifs in materials such as cast stone or stone. This much is evident from Michelangelo's unbuilt facade designed for San Lorenzo, Florence, among other proposals. While Semper's theorization of tectonics resoundingly concludes the classical period of architecture, it simultaneously inaugurates the crisis of fabrication in modern times, when new materials and construction techniques demand a different art-form. The appropriateness of iron and steel for the expressive dimension of monumentality triggered a hot debate among nineteenth-century architects and historians. There lies the historical significance of Le Corbusier's Five Points of Architecture and Mies van der Rohe's radical recoding of the Semperian tectonics. This involved the recognition of the "criterion of the 'minimal'" so important to iron, to recall Benjamin. The constructive structure of the frame, each of these architects formulated, "includes the minimal element of quantity; the 'little,' the 'few.'" Benjamin continues, "These are dimensions that were well established in technological and architectural construction long before literature made bold to adopt them. Fundamentally, it is the question of the earliest manifestation of the principle of montage."[22] Accordingly, we need to re-interpret the Semperian tectonics that architecture is construction plus something else. This added something else (cladding or covering) opens a space for the representational continuity of classical architecture, knowing that Semper shunned using iron for civic architecture. Interestingly enough, this suggested excess has turned out to be the core crisis of contemporary architecture, wherein digital reproducibility has ushered in the art-form's total technification,[23] an aestheticization associable with the spectacle of the commodity form. Surprisingly, similar to the essential elements of the classical language of architecture, in most digitally reproduced architecture, the skin is fabricated independently and anchored to the body of the building. It seems Semper may have seen this urge for science and technology coming when he announced that "the more we advance in civilization and science, the more it seems that that instinctive feeling, which men followed in their first attempts in their industrial arts, loses its strength, ..."[24] As such, we could argue that the art-form in Semper's tectonics aimed at reiterating the importance of the symbolic (representational) dimension of architecture in a more "advanced" stage of civilization. It was a strategy of resistance proper to architecture, a cultural product with expanded ties to science and technology evident even at the dawn of the industrial revolution, the 1850s. In fact, similar to others in London at the time, Semper had the opportunity to see the differences between hand-made utensils and machines as the agency of commodification and abstraction closely. Semper's thesis of the Four Elements of Architecture, I argue, underlines architecture's direct or indirect affiliation with labor, industry, and material transformation (*Stoffwechsel*) discussed in this book's chapters. In passing, Semper's use of *Stoffwechsel* should be understood as a sensuous "relationality of forces, and it is as appropriation that is the condition and possibility of production."[25] Thus, the criticality of "active intuition" for a sensuous appropriation of motifs transformed from each of the four industries towards the production of architecture.

Towards the end of his preface to the first English edition of Semper's London lecture, written during the architect's stay in England, Joseph Rykwert suggests that Semper's museum-designed work "could remake his consciousness and his body in the image of his primal house. He could, therefore, feel himself becoming an architect through contemplation of his own body."[26] It is not hard to speculate on whether Rykwert's juxtaposition between "museum" and the primal house was an analogy to the Crystal Palace and Caribbean hut. In any event, what interests us is that the labor involved in each of the four industries mentioned in Semper's lecture leaves a mark on the maker and the spectator's self-cultivation.

This has as much to do with the break between art and craft inherent in the development of nineteenth-century "arts and manufacturers" as the "decisive break between man the tool-maker and man the image-maker."[27] Thus, the subjective formation as part of practice: "the knot in wall decoration, the stroke of the axe or chisel on the wood, the hammer on the stone, the molding hand on the clay." Rykwert's interest in the corporeal analogy between the body and *building* allowed him to bypass the core-form and art-form divide central to tectonics. In this, he resonates Semper's description of the Greek temples and monuments that were not constructed or ornamented but emerged as "organic life produced when counteracting and struggling against gravity and substance."[28] Linking beauty with "necessity," Semper presented an alternative to the nineteenth-century debate on the ornament as either an addition to a constructed form or evolving in the construction process. For Semper, necessity was the lawful articulation of the object to the satisfaction of both the maker and the user. More interesting and concerning the idea of theatricality is Semper's reflection on the Greeks' analogical use of the human form supporting the entablature. According to him, this was not an aberration but a conscious attempt at "animating the architectural parts themselves instead of decorating them with ornamental applications taken from the organic nature, as Egyptians did."[29]

The notion of animation is implied in Semper's distinction between the core-form and the art-form. It is also suggested in transforming motifs from applied art objects to architecture. However, animation attains its full manifestation in the spectacular surface appearance of contemporary architecture itself, a commodity form among other commodities permeating everyday life. Semper could not see this coming, a limitation he overcomes with his insightful observation of the animation inherent in the material transformation of rope into the materiality of a knot (Figure 1.5), the Semperian analog for detailing in architecture. Animation is also implied in the wreath, an archetypal work of art using various materials, techniques, and skills to make a textile piece. Should we push the envelope further and compare the transformation of the rope to a knot with Marx's discussion of the expressive dramatization (theatricalization?) involved in the transformation of the "relative value-form" of the linen into the commodity form of a coat?[30] As we will see in the labor chapter, thanks to the culture of Humanism, architectural art-form disguises the fabrication

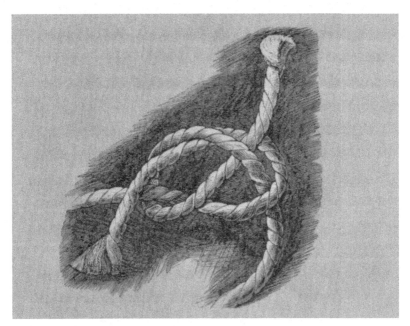

Figure 1.5 Knot, Gottfried Semper, Der Stil, 1860.

Source: Image courtesy of Getty Research Institute, Los Angeles.

labor, making the work's appearance a source of visual pleasure in analogy to the human body and with the sea of commodities today.

Semper's deliberation on the importance of applied arts for architecture concerns two ideas: in the first place, it is the unity between use, material, and artifacts of daily use, which most often have a close affiliation with the body. Second, because of their longevity, most applied art objects' surface embellishment codifies the symbolic (collective) dimension of a given cultural evolution within a particular geographic region. This much is evident from Semper's characterization of the Egyptian situla compared to the Greek hydria, one shaped to get water from a river and carried on yokes (Figure 1.6) and the other shaped to catch water from a fountain, evident in the funnel-shaped feature of its mouth and the neck. To further highlight Semper's comparison of these two vessels, we should recall Karl Kraus and Adolf Loos's demonstrations, one literally and the

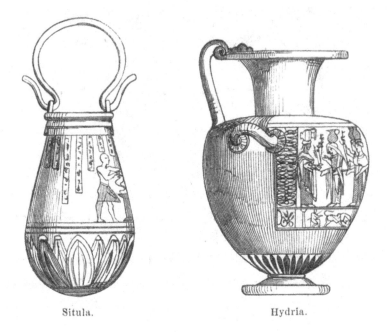

Situla.   Hydria.

Figure 1.6 Situla and hydria, Gottfried Semper, Der Stil, 1860.

Source: Image courtesy of Getty Research Institute, Los Angeles.

other in words, that "there is a difference between an urn and a chamber pot, and that it is this difference that provides the scope of culture to develop."[31] Similarly, Semper argued that an unmovable work (building?) should show its differences from a moveable object, anticipating Loos' emphasis on the expressive "purpose" of the work, explored in his article on the principle of dressing. Semper similarly could not but agree with Loos' critique of the aesthetic of abstraction permeating the architecture of early modernism, exemplified in Le Corbusier's early villas, even though both architects shun the use of ornament for different reasons. Loos was also critical of the abstraction in utilitarian objects designed and produced by the Bauhaus school agency.[32] Likewise, Semper could see how the machine inserts a space between the maker and the object, enticing the former to comprehend the object as a spectator, visual, or otherwise. The implied divide slowly but surely transmitted various fabrication elements to the machine and machine-made materials with no role in traditional utensils. There is another dimension to the divide between the maker and the object worth reiterating here. I have already mentioned the intimate relationship between the body and various artifacts, useful utensils, tools, and clothing since ancient times. Particular to these artifacts was an aura that, during the age of mechanical reproducibility, was subdued by the fetishism of commodities, as Marx elaborated in the first volume of *Das Kapital*. The abstraction involved in the object's transformation from use value to exchange value "consumes ever more concrete human bodies."[33] Writing on the state of "design" since 1750, Adrian Forty correctly observes that most studies focus on the design's attempt to make the object beautiful, while few studies go further to establish the design's "connections to the brain and the pocket."[34] The economic dimension of this observation fits well with Marx's experience, for example, his musings on how to receive money from a pawned coat, mentioned earlier in this essay.[35] For Marx, a jacket is a matter of prestige and identity while satisfying a desire to look nice and wear good attire. There is nothing wrong with this aspect of human desire; however, since the commodification of objects, the problem is that the design's look has been charged with *excess*, enticing one to desire objects beyond his/her pocket and necessity. This is the fetishism of commodities that has also been infused into contemporary architecture, whether it is a residential, commercial, or civic building. This is also the core of the architectural crisis today, and I would claim that Semper offers lenses for understanding and critiquing this phenomenon. I also want to argue that the dual nature of fabrics used to separate spaces is central to Semper's radicalism, which should be extended to Loos. This Viennese architect treated the interior cladding of the walls (*Bekleidung*), floors, and ceilings, to create a sensual space central to the domestic environment's pre-modern experience, in contrast to the exterior walls that he believed belonged to the metropolis.[36] The same distinction is implied in Semper's discussion of the fabric's essentiality for covering the space occupied by the body. Playing with the etymology of the German words *Wand* (wall) and *Gewand* (garment), he suggested that the hard stone and masonry behind the fabric were to protect the interior space from wind and other external issues such as security threats, and, due to time and technical developments, these surfaces were articulated by patterns developed in weaving, textiles, and carpet in particular. These aspects of Semper's "four elements" are part of the reason why his theorization of architecture has become topical in the course of the last two decades. In the following, I want to demonstrate the animation involved in Semper's tectonic theory and propose an alternative understanding of theatricality that differentiates it from theatricalization, the spectacle enforced by digital reproducibility.

Semper's impulse in underlining the critical importance of the motifs developed in the applied arts for the art-form of the building was not nostalgic, as was the case with most of his London colleagues who upheld the ethos of the Arts and Crafts movement. We can trace Semper's radical and constructivist approach in his London lecture and throughout *Der Stil* (the 1860s). Demonstrating examples of wall clothing from the ancient world, he was convinced that the fabricators followed the principles of the tapestry. His motto was "how to change old forms, consecrated by necessity and tradition, according to our new means of fabrication."[37] We are reminded of the early use of bronze for coating wooden doors and how the later material and technical transformations facilitated the fabrication of doors made out of bronze. At the time of writing these words, Semper might have known that technological advances made it possible, for example, "to sheathe cast iron with copper, a process which must not be abused,"[38] as part of the Semperian lawful masking of the surface of an artifact. This led Semper to theorize the ornament-structure dialogue evident in Assyrian furniture work, while still recalling that the Persian column, a wooden shaft coated by metal plates with weaker symbolic elements drawn from Assyrian furniture, was a step toward transforming the wooden core's function to the surrounding shell, and its final elimination. Thus, writes Semper, "the 'structural scheme' and the 'artistic scheme' become one, and the organic idea that would find its ideal application in Greece is already a reality here." The excited Semper proclaimed that "Everything is ready; all that is needed is the animating spark of Prometheus!"[39] The suggested "organic idea" refers to the realization of Greek and Persian stone columns, with the difference that the latter's capital imitated the original form of the metal plates covering its wooden shaft. In these examples, theatricality is involved in a constructivist transformation of metal plates into stone, with improvements in labor and skills needed to give the stone a desirable shape.

Crisis of the Column and Wall

Notwithstanding Semper's reservations about iron's suitability for civic architecture, he could not dismiss the animating spark of Prometheus in the Crystal Palace. In many ways, the structure of the Great Exhibition was the harbinger of what to expect from the rising young capitalism in England, the heartland of textile industries. With a *big* panoramic interior space, the building legitimized the art of engineering beyond matters concerning science and technology. It condoned the specter of the fetishism of the displayed commodities, old, and new. The structure was also emblematic of what Semper would agree and disagree with in the work of archaeologist Carl Bötticher, author of *Die Tektonik der Hellenen* (1844–52). Semper read this book's first edition at the British Museum in London. According to Wolfgang Hermann, Semper was surprised to find their commonalities, to the point that he felt comfortable using Bötticher's axiomatic differentiation between core-form and art-form (*Kern-und Kunst-form*) from then on.[40] Hermann elaborates on the four basic differences between these two German tectonic theorists[41]; however, here, we will only highlight how their take on tectonics anticipated the emerging state of the tectonics of the column and wall.

Semper's prioritization of motifs developed in textiles, and their subsequent use for the space-covering elements did indeed establish the essentiality of the wall for the representational dimension of tectonics. Still, this does not mean that the column had no place in Semper's tectonic thinking. Rather, his analytical exploration of columns in Assyrian, Egyptian, Persian, and Greek architecture was to reaffirm his understanding of the core-form and art-form divide. Discussing the influence of costumes on architecture, Semper speculated that most structural symbols utilized in architecture, such as the ornaments used in Egyptian capitals, were motifs borrowed from Egyptian ladies' hair decoration.[42] For Bötticher, by contrast, the core-form/art-form divide was emblematized by the Greek temple, a higher state of masonry (stone?) construction system with no influences from outside nor from other cultures or industries. In the Greek temple, he wrote, the dressing was conceived simultaneously with the configuration of the core-form, the mechanical function.[43] The double curvature molding of the Doric cyma, for example, was a symbol of load and support, "a seam within the structure signifying the notions of upright-standing and free-finishing," writes Harry-Francis Mallgrave.[44] For Bötticher, the Doric and the Ionic orders were "independent styles," with symbols that "had originally been created for stone building; they had not been taken over from an earlier fictitious building made from wood."[45] This makes sense following Auguste Choisy's notion of "a timber masonry," which, according to Joseph Rykwert, "seemed to reconcile the conflicting accounts of the timber origin of the orders with the demands of stone construction." Choisy's *History of Architecture* (1899), Rykwert continues, was an essential read for Auguste Perret and Le Corbusier.[46] In any event, Bötticher's position was partly in dismissal of Semper, who argued for the influences of the so-called barbarians on Greek architecture. Accordingly, it's not farfetched to suggest that tectonics in Semper's theorization of architecture drew from the Renaissance. In almost all pre-modern buildings, the surface articulations, particularly the rapport between column and wall, benefited from Leon Battista Alberti, for whom the column was an ornament par excellence.[47] The columns inscribed in the Palazzo Rucellai's facade were to animate and lessen the monotony of the surface of a flat masonry wall.

Considering various theorizations of ornament in the nineteenth century, the column and wall in Rucellai are in accord with the Semperian notion of tectonic theatricality (lawful animation of the constructed form) despite Alberti's presentation of the column as an ornament, but also because in this case the *ornament* was neither addition nor emerged as part of the construction process. In passing, I must say that this reading of the Renaissance discourse on the column and the wall is retrospective and interpretative in the light of Semper's theorization of architecture rather than semantic (structuralist) as exemplified in Hubert Damisch's eloquent discussion of the subject referenced below. Damisch writes that the column as ornament takes on a different function from the mechanical one assigned in a skeleton system. In the Albertian system, the column "assumes the values of a sign within" the Saussurian syntagmatic and paradigmatic system.[48]

However, the column and wall had already attained a certain degree of expressive figuration in Roman architectural works, the Colosseum for one, even though their symbols were initially produced in textiles or other applied art objects. What I am driving at is this: unlike Bötticher, Semper's theorization of tectonics was historical through and through. Architecture is not an autonomous state of thinking and making developed in isolation from other production activities and without borrowing from different cultures' art-forms.[49] The comparative history of architecture underpinning Semper's discourse is heard loud and clear in his critique of speculative intellectualism. He writes of a "speculative philosophy of art [that] dreams of an ideal Doric scheme that has not evolved historically" but has come about through a "legendary miraculous birth."[50] While Semper here sounds globalist, Bötticher's obsession with the intellectual capacity of the Hellenes aside, his position on tectonics surprisingly comes closer to contemporary readings of tectonics, Frampton's "poetics of construction"[51] in particular.

Interestingly enough, in his 1846 speech, Bötticher claimed that the two major masonry tectonics that evolved in Greek and Gothic architecture had exhausted the potentialities of stone tectonics and that a new system for covering space rested on the strength of iron.[52] A similar speculative position was raised by Benjamin without him being familiar with Bötticher's text. We have already noted Benjamin's views on iron and nineteenth century's engineering achievements as the messengers of the coming epoch. In contrast to both Greek and Gothic stone construction and the related ceiling systems, Benjamin claimed that a "new and unprecedented ceiling system, one that will naturally bring in its wake a whole new realm of art forms, can ... make its appearance only after some particular material—formerly neglected, if not unknown, as a basic principle in that application—begins to be accepted." He ends this statement by saying that such material is iron.[53] With its astonishing results in engineering work, and its topicality in the 1880s for its architectural possibilities, iron did not have enough body, or matter conducive to architectural expression, to recall Semper.[54] Again, Benjamin reminds us that "Iron inspired a certain distrust just because it was not immediately furnished by nature, but instead had to be artificially prepared as a building material."[55] Thus, the argument that the historicity of the Crystal Palace, a hinge between Semper and Bötticher's discourse on tectonics, and the turn from masonry construction to the steel and glass system, was the way forward. There is a historiographic dimension to this proclamation; elsewhere,[56] I have argued that the dichotomy between the element of the wall enclosure and the frame tectonics is central to Frampton's position on the possible expansion of the modernist project on architecture. His stance is in sharp contrast to Francesco Dal Co and Tafuri's sympathy with Mies's work, wherein the most meaningful attributes of the Semperian art-form are narrowed to the tectonic implications of the nihilism of modernity.

The Crystal Palace also consolidated the myth of the primitive hut, a wooden structure comprising four columns and a roof covering the space marked by its four supports, with no enclosure. As such, the hut was repetitively presented in most reflections on the origins of architecture, exemplified in Marc-Antoine Laugier's cover page for

Essai sur l'architecture (1755),[57] the closest to Semper's time. According to Laugier, "It is by approaching the simplicity of this model that fundamental mistakes are avoided." Again, we might think of Mies's late work, which is erroneously associated with the aesthetic of minimalism of the late 1960s. In any event, the juxtaposition of the primitive hut with the Miesian steel and glass architecture suggests the singular visibility of the column even many centuries after the realization of the Greek temple. By singular, I refer to the column's dissociation and departure from its tectonic rapport with the wall, evident even in the columnar system of the Greek temple, and mediating between the external space and the interior of the walled *cella*, the hearth (the statue of a deity), the spiritual cluster of the temple. In addition to its load-carrying function, the column does not enclose anything; on the contrary, the column is the "precise opposite of an interior closed on all sides" by a wall.[58] From a Hegelian perspective, the Greek temple represents the highest symbolic rapport between the column and wall, evaporated immediately after the removal of the enclosed sculpture, and displayed in public as a work of art in itself. I have no intention of discussing the many implications of Hegel's aesthetics here.[59] It is enough to highlight another moment in architecture's history when the column also stands apart from the wall, enclosing the space of the Pantheon, Jacques-Germain Soufflot's Church of Sainte-Genevieve, Paris, 1755–90.

Most images taken from the interior space of the church of Ste Genevieve (also known as the Pantheon) focus on a free-standing classical column (Figure 1.7). The image discloses a departure from the expected traditional aesthetics wherein a free-standing column is positioned next to a pier and a wall.[60] An exception to this tectonic generalization is the Doric temple at Paestum, which Soufflot had visited in 1750. Surrounded by free-standing Doric columns on four sides, the temple raised the problem of the corner column, the architectonics of which have been revisited by many architects since then. The tectonic rapport between the aesthetic and the structural (image) is suggested by Bergdoll: he writes, "Soufflot's project was continuously revised and refined over the long years of construction, marking it as the foremost of several experimental buildings where the aesthetic and structural limits of architecture were tested and debated."[61] The design of Ste Genevieve uniquely combined what we might call structural clarity with spatial lucidity, even though it was achieved by a system of hidden iron rods reinforcing the building's vaults. Still, the "free-standing" interior columns of the Church of Ste Genevieve allude to a fundamental departure from the Vitruvian

Figure 1.7 Jacques-Germain Soufflot, Sainte Genevieve, Paris, 1755–90 (interior view).

Source: Photo courtesy of Wikimedia Commons, the free media repository.

association of the column with the human body and from the concept of the Orders—the progenitor of the classical language of architecture—which overshadowed architectural praxis until the dawn of the industrial revolution and the subsequent emergence of the need for new and unprecedented building types. Here is what Antoine Picon has to say on this subject: according to him, the building "disregarded established rules about proportions, such as those between the span of arches and the width of the corresponding piers, and between the diameter of a cupola and the thickness of the pillars supporting it." Picon concludes, "this change would enable the emergence of the notion of structure alongside its gradual dissociation from ornament."[62] At an abstract intellectual level, yes, Soufflot's free-standing classical column was the progenitor of the modern steel structural system, anticipating J.-N.-L. Durand's idea of the grid's role in laying out a design that ridicules any attempt to associate architecture with the human body.[63] Analogically, however, the same column's tectonic articulations attempted to "resume the authoritative clothes of the past so as to create authority in the present."[64] As an individual element, Soufflot's column neither departed from the classical three-parts composition nor relinquished its classical rapport with the wall, a linguistic syntax. What its free-standing posture does is to bring to visibility what has been, in the classical syntax of column and wall, the invisibility of "enclosure" that demarcates the duality between interior and exterior. In the Pantheon, the wall provides an appropriate enclosure for the space ordered by free-standing columns. Accordingly, the column and the wall departed from the syntax codified in Roman and Greek architecture, respectively. In this transaction, the column had to be conceived of as an Albertian ornament in order to retain a different rapport with the wall,[65] which paradoxically is not identical to the wall in Roman architecture. The individuated column with a circular section demonstrates that it "only acts as a support on its own account and that, unlike a square pillar, it does not lend itself to forming a continuous wall through adhesion."[66] From this point to the Miesian "naked" column removed away from the corner, there was progressive dilapidation of the classical tectonics of column and wall, which attained its modernist figuration in Le Corbusier's Dom-ino frame. Mapped along with the Albertian problem of column and wall, the frame concepts pursued by Mies and Le Corbusier give the order "systematize architecture."[67]

Was the deconstructivist strategy evident in the Miesian take on the column—its separation from the enclosure wall and the column's move away from the corner—a tectonic hinge that solidified the autonomy of the facade in the classical masonry architecture that was conceived in analogy to the body? On the other hand, the over-presence of the roof and the column in Mies' later work confirms the hut, Caribbean or otherwise, as the tectonic model. At one point, Mies might have realized that the masonry wall was initially used as an enclosure element rather than tectonic, as with the Greek temple. A diagram drawing of the plan of the temple demonstrates an abstract composition of points (columns) and lines (walls), one articulating spatial intervals (openings) dictated by mechanical knowledge of antiquity, while the other marks territorial differences between inside and outside. If the wooden post was the tectonic ancestor of the column, tectonic plate movement should be considered the model for the linear nature of the wall as a delineating element attaining constructive visibility since the Roman territorial subdivision and walling system. According to Bernard Cache, "Architecture would be the art of introducing intervals in a territory in order to construct frames of probability." Out of the three functions he charts for the realization of architecture, the wall is the first functional element for separation and "the basis of our coexistence," he claims.[68] Despite their ontological difference, the architectonic unfolding of such a coexistence necessitates the dialectical rapport between the column and the wall pursued paradigmatically by Alberti and Mies. And despite Adolf Loos' and Louis I. Khan's resentment of using the column in most of their work (to mention two architects from the historical panorama of modern architecture), the significance of the crisis of the column and the wall, as discussed here, is relevant to the architecture's contemporaneity. For example, after Mies, neither postmodernist architecture nor the digitally reproduced architecture with its esteem for the surface covering has shown an interest in tectonics. At its best moment, the latter is a reminder of the tent as an atectonic model, at the expense of the essentiality of the tectonics of column and wall.

Technification of Architecture

Within the gamut of modernism, Mies and Le Corbusier institutionalized two different lexicons of architecture and inaugurated the path to de- and reterritorializing the building culture of Humanism. With full awareness and knowledge of architectural history, these two architects' linguistic economy was vigorous and systematic. Like the "twelfth-century substitution of ribbed vaults for compound vaults," Mies and Le Corbusier formulated the architecture of uneven temporalities in contradistinction to historicism (postmodernism) and the latest new design (parametric). Neither of these latter tendencies has been able to systemize architecture within the long history of modern architecture without borrowing classical and futuristic garments, sidestepping *construction* indispensable to the building art. Where these two tendencies' work "irritates, sharpens conflict, deliberately confuses," critical practice today should establish a sensible relationship between action (design) and the work. According to Rykwert, the solution to the contemporary predicament of architecture is not the "unfettered development of technology" or the "statistical musings of behavioral scientists."[69] With these observations in mind, I would like to highlight the importance of Semper's theorization of architecture for a critique of architecture's contemporaneity, which seemingly has chosen the path of the "technification" of architecture, mindful of the historical avant-garde rhetoric.

The two concepts of the frame Le Corbusier and Mies championed have remained essential for contemporary architecture, despite or because of architecture's turn to digital reproducibility circa the 1990s. The Dom-ino and the Miesian frame responded to modernity's core conviction, which was by no means anti-historical, but aimed at recoding the past culture of building without discarding the emerging everyday life and technical achievements accumulated since the late eighteenth century in Europe. They were also responding to the institutionalization of architecture's educational system in contra-distinction to that of engineering, highlighting the visibility of the culture of building roughly in 1756. This date coincides with Marc-Antoine Laugier's publication of *Essai sur l'Architecture* in 1755. The image of the hut used for the book's cover page presents, as noted above, a positivistic notion of four supporting columns defining the space while holding the roof up. His was a generic type (model) of structural organization contrary to Semper's tectonics. The difference rests on the notion of the culture of building, which comprises knowledge of the matter, material, and its metamorphosis to materiality, and the recognition of architecture as *language* starting with Vitruvius's theorization of the Five Orders. According to Semper, the skills and knowledge informing the motifs developed in carpentry and textiles were essential for the architectonics of the column and walls. Yet, the wooden column of the imaginary hut had to be re-coded anew using stone, with embellishments evident in each of the classical five orders and the Roman walls. A similar transformative process was involved in changing the motifs of fabric into stone or brick walls, a subject Semper elaborates on in detail. Using ashlar and brick (Figure 2.1), the pre-modern culture of building endowed buildings with various surface embellishments and detailing, to be re-coded when industrial materials such as iron, glass, and concrete became available. The structural frame system conceived by Mies and Le Corbusier encapsulates the historicity of the suggested transformations.

Still, while engineers had already produced dazzling structures during the eighteenth century, prompting Sigfried Giedion to remind architects of their task ahead, architects had no choice but to wait until the time arrived. Whereas scientific and mathematical developments were essential for engineering, architects could not but stick to the inherited masonry culture of building's technical knowledge and skills for some time. A limitation, if you like, that did not stop Le Corbusier's exaltation of the engineer in the opening pages of *Vers une Architecture* (Paris, 1924) in words such as "looking ahead a bit." Le Corbusier was also inspired by Russian Constructivists, a body of work that inspired Benjamin, who also praised Le Corbusier. Benjamin had this to say about the early dichotomy between architecture and engineering: "For in those days who besides the engineer and the proletarian had climbed the steps that alone made it possible to recognize what was new and decisive about these structures: the feeling of space."[70] The juxtaposition of the emerging two figures was the raw material for Benjamin to postulate that each age sees the next one in their dreams! On another occasion, Le Corbusier wrote, "I would soon have a premonition of 'the constructor,' the new man for a new age."[71] There seems to be an auspice arrangement between his image of "the new man" and the Dom-ino frame. Frampton writes, "Veering away from his aspiration to become a high bourgeois architect, Jeanneret concentrated, at this stage of his development, on the rationalization of building production, particularly as it might be applied to low-cost housing."[72] The Dom-ino project (1915) was indeed a step towards the rationalization of the production of architecture that inevitably had to be geared with relevant technical unfolding in most trades involved in the production process of architecture. We are reminded of not only the Case Study Houses, including Charles and Ray Eames' House No. 8, California (1940s), which combined prefabricated panels with a steel frame system but also, Walter Gropius and Konrad Wachsmann's Panel House system of 1942, design ideas that had been developing since the inauguration of the Bauhaus school in 1919. In this line of consideration, we might also add Buckminister Fuller's research, publications, and structures delivering practical and inexpensive shelters in the spirit of engineering.

And yet, among many other impressive technically motivated designs, Le Corbusier and Mies's frame remains unique for many reasons, including the fact that they emerged from the backbone of pre-modern building culture, posthumous to the required developments in the science of mechanics, and the accumulated practical experience exemplified in the late nineteenth-century engineering structures. Organizing his notes on the subject of iron for *The Arcades Project*, Benjamin penned that no one in the past knew how to build with glass and iron. The problem "has long since been solved by hangars and silos."[73] What stands out in the work of Mies and Le Corbusier is two different re-thinking of the rapport between the column and the wall. Studying Hadrian's Villa in Rome, Le Corbusier noted that architecture "has as its goal to make us cheerful or serene. Have respect for walls. Pompeian does not put holes in his walls; he has devotion for walls, a love for light." He continued, "the *impression* of light extends beyond through cylinders (I do not like to say *columns*, the word has been spoiled), peristyle, or pillars."[74] Thus, transfiguring the column in the Dom-ino frame into a structural system re-territorializing the Renaissance notion of the facade. Since then, the wall has been chiefly conceived as a free-facade, or space partitioning element. Elsewhere, I have discussed Mies's early experimentation with brick, concrete, and glass, culminating in his 1930s brick-courtyard houses, a body of work revisited in the Barcelona Pavilion's column and tectonics, doing away with both the loadbearing and expressive potentialities of the wall. Considering these two architects' early and late work, it's not farfetched to say that the Domino frame is the hidden structure beneath the surface articulation of most contemporary architecture. On the other hand, the Miesian skin and bone overshadow the best work of Renzo Piano, Richard Rogers, and Norman Foster, among others.[75]

The expressed high steam for the legacy of Mies and Le Corbusier in contemporary architecture is convincing, particularly regarding the question of technology, a central issue for the formation of modern architecture, and the predicament of contemporary architecture. To recall the opening of this essay, I shall limit the following pages to Martin Heidegger's "The Question Concerning Technology" and Theodor Adorno's notion of technification. For reasons elaborated below, we cannot do justice to these two positions without considering Benjamin's "exhibition value of the work," discussed in his famous essay "The Work of Art in the Age of Mechanical Reproducibility." The reader might recall this author's engagement with Benjamin's work on numerous occasions; here, I intend to associate the "exhibition value" with the Semperian distinction between theatricalization and the tectonic of theatricality. This is important because technology underpins both notions of theatricalization and exhibition value, as discussed by Semper and Benjamin, respectively.

Heidegger wrote "The Question Concerning Technology" before the date of its first presentation in 1949. Starting with the essentiality of "cause and effect" for most human activities, Heidegger outlines "four causalities" that brought together the Greek Temple. Accordingly, "the four causes are the ways, all belonging to each other, of being responsible for something else."[76] To solidify the argument that the logos of science primarily consummates the essence of technology in modernity, Heidegger reminds us of the Greek word *Technikon* and its etymological root, *techne*, the art of making, poiesis. At the time of writing his essay, Heidegger, like most phenomenological thinkers,[77] was convinced of the impossibility of poiesis in modern times because technology "reveals" how both nature and other elements that give order to everyday life are now "standing in reserve" to be consumed by the instrumental logic of modern technology. His timely critique of technology during the war years aside, the problem with Heidegger's argument was to associate the "true" essence of technology with the once-upon-a-time Greek aura, thus presenting a ghostly vision of history contrary to the Marxian progressive concept of history "oriented toward a futurity conceived as the essential difference from the presence."[78] Similar to the writings of other phenomenologists of the time, Heidegger's lamentation for a situation when tools were conceived adjunct to human labor "paradoxically renders the past immensely more present at the same time that it is invisible, having been effaced in the process by its own 'extinguishing.'" Fredric Jamerson continues, "Heidegger's anti-modernism ... cannot imagine a solution to technological alienation except by way of regression,"[79] like that already manifested in the Ruskinian call for a return to the medieval guild system.

Despite this and similar criticisms, several architects and historians embraced Heidegger's views on technology and dwelling during the 1970s, most likely because, towards the end of his take on technology, the philosopher mused that art and architecture's affiliation with *techne* could launch a critique of the modern essence of technology. Interestingly enough, the German edition of Heidegger's text, published in 1954, a decade after the publication of Adorno and Max Horkheimer's "The Culture Industry: Enlightenment as Mass Deception," a chapter in *Dialectic of Enlightenment*, 1944. While sympathetic to the Heideggerian notion of the thingness of the work of art, what underpins Adorno's take on art and technology, discussed in numerous essays, is the contention that "The modernity of art lies in its mimetic relation to a petrified and alienated reality,"[80] the prevailing objectivity of the commodity form. For Adorno, there are two aspects to the work of art, "being both an autonomous entity and a social fact." To further elucidate this point, it is crucial to reiterate Adorno's position on the dialectics of art and technique, both social facts in their own right; however, since the instrumental logic of technology has been accepted as a matter of fact since the late nineteenth century, it is useful to discuss the relationship between architecture and technique in analogy to Adorno's reflection on music.

The analogy is useful, recalling Semper, who compared architecture's cosmic dimension with music and dance rather than representational arts. For Adorno, the compositional balance between "the content of notes and the sensuously reproducing sounds" vanishes when the composition is overdetermined by techniques that "had developed outside music in the course of the general growth of technology."[81] A similar unfolding informs the present situation where the aesthetic of commodity form has taken over the cultural realm. We must thus argue that a critical praxis should focus on tech-nification, a symptom of the infusion of technology into most cultural products, architecture included. This transformation writes Andreas Huyssen, "completed with the stage of monopoly capitalism, reaches so deep that the Marxian separation of economy and culture as base and superstructure is itself is called into question."[82] Accordingly, a different spirit of the time is revealed, wherein "without being con-scious of society, ... the work of art, and notably, music which is far removed from concepts, represent society."[83] Adorno extends his critical remarks on Richard Wagner, who knew Semper, to include jazz, which to him would have been less appealing if its sound was not mediated by technological means. Through the concept of the technification of music, Adorno suggests that the dialectical relation-ship between content and technique is jeopardized when a musician adopts means that are not derived from composition in the first place. Regarding compositions assisted by electronic means, he believed that "The whole official musical culture is moving in the direction of fetishizing of means, and is even celebrating a triumph among its enemies in the avant-garde."[84] His observations initiated the drive for a strategic concept of autonomy, necessitating a dialectical under-standing of distanciation and engagement with the prevailing state of the commodity form, a position Benjamin also subscribed to, not-withstanding Adorno's reservations about Benjamin's discourse on technology.

Written in 1935, Benjamin's essay "The Work of Art in the Age of Mechanical Reproduction" discusses the impact of technology on human perception.[85] Presenting the case of montage in film, Benjamin put forward the idea of "wish-images" in conjunction with the loss of aura; that is, the magical and ritualistic origin of the work of art where space and time are intermingled, and harmony between the desire of the subject and the skills of the hand prevails. On another occasion, Benjamin describes the idea of aura in the follow-ing words: in a strange weave of space and time: the unique appear-ance or resemblance of distance, no matter how close the object may be. While resting on a summer's noon, to trace a range of mountains on the horizon or a branch that throws its shadow on the observer until the moment or the hour becomes part of their appearance—that is what it means to breathe the aura of those mountains.[86] If, for Benjamin, modernity was a departure from the auratic experi-ence of time and space, Heidegger intended to critique the instru-mental logic of technology to recollect the presumed being and time of the auratic experience. More important again are the political connotations of their views. Notwithstanding Heidegger's position, Benjamin believed that the existing differences between the working class and artists are "superficial in a world of transformed skills and socialized technology."[87] His aim was not to return to any bygone past but to look forward to a situation similar to what he penned in his Moscow Diaries.[88]

Now, with Benjamin distancing himself from historicism and discussing architecture in the light of the work's tactile and optical dimensions, it is equally important to notice that his discourse on historical material alludes to a shift from an individual to a collective experience of a past not necessarily embedded in high art, but instead resting in anonymous works and details. This attention to the marginal was, for Benjamin, the result of a significant methodological discovery laid down in Alois Riegl's *Late Roman Art Industry*, where the art historian "broke with the theory of 'periods of decline,' in recognition of what had previously been called 'regression into barbarism' a new experience of space, a new artistic volition [*kunstwollen*]."[89] This much is also evident from Semper's break away from the classical wisdom of architecture, locating the origin of monuments in marginal works like the stage sets for carnivals and skills developed in textiles, carpentry, ceramics, and masonry, as mentioned earlier.[90] Interestingly, Benjamin highlights the principle of montage, a means to "build up the large constructions out of the smallest, precisely fashioned structural elements. Indeed, to detect the crystal of the total event in the analysis of the small, individual moment."[91] To see the archaic in the latest technologies, as Benjamin suggested, shows a strategic position radically different from Heidegger, while at the same time, questioning the linear idea of progress without dismissing the radical potentialities of the new techniques. However, what makes Benjamin relevant to the main subject of this essay is his insightful approach to the techniques in modern arts and the work of Le Corbusier and Loos. Equally important is his method of delivering a critical strategy unavailable to most critics and historians writing before the post-war era, which implicitly highlights the importance of "construction" for modern art and architecture. The aim is also to address "construction" within a theoretical paradigm that juxtaposes Benjamin's discourse on the exhibition value of the art and Semper's notion of theatricality.[92]

Benjamin's essay also maps the vicissitudes of the crisis of the object in modernity. Towards the end of the article, he reflects on architecture without providing a detailed account of the impact of technology on it. Benjamin's belief that buildings are appropriated by habit and tactile experience shows the complexities involved in the idea of the crisis of the object. For Benjamin, architecture provides a reception model comparable to film, where "the distracted mass absorbs the work of art." This aspect of the film, he writes, "is most obvious concerning buildings. Architecture has always represented the prototype of a work of art, the reception of which is consummated by a collective in a state of distraction."[93] There are two conclusions we should draw from Benjamin's observation. First, the most enduring elements of architecture embrace both construction and aesthetics. This is not to say that the historically received forms and typologies should be imitated as written rules. Instead, these formal structures should be re-coded as "handing over" the building culture to the modernization process. More importantly, how to assess Benjamin's conviction that after the loss of aura, the work of art seized every opportunity to display its exhibitionist value, an aesthetic sensibility that has been formative, on and off, for the crisis since the rise of modern movement architecture? If the distraction Benjamin alludes to relates to the Metropolis's everyday experience, should architecture not resist this experience? Paradoxically, architecture has no choice but to emulate, if not internalize, some aspects of that experience, which is in tune with the ideological temperament of capitalism.[94] I would like to posit that distraction finds its architectonic form in the fragmentation and juxtaposition of dreamlike forms with familiar tectonics that can be mistaken for Semper's discourse on theatricality.

Semper is topical today not because the fabric of covering can be reproduced digitally but because the tectonic is a cosmic art in which the art-form relates to the core-form in "a *structural-symbolic* rather than in a *structural-technical* sense."[95] The perceived duality in the tectonic not only attests to the in-between state of architecture (compared to the opposition between art and craft and the work of engineering) but also marks a departure from the classical *techné* by which the homology between the technical, symbolic, and aesthetic of architecture was secured. What is involved here is the possibility of radicalizing Semper's theory further, and claim that after the mechanical reproducibility of art, but also facing the contemporary drive for fragmentation and image making, the tectonic should stress the perceived spatial envelope as a lawful fabrication, an artifice as Semper would say. When this is established, the question would be: how and to what end is it beneficial to advance an argument to distinguish between theatricalization and the tectonic of theatricality?[96] The Semperian distinction between the core-form and the art-form introduces a rift that should be reconceived in tectonic form.

Otherwise, in the light of the present spectacle culture, the art-form is presented as an autonomous cool fabric, suited to the touristic appreciation of architecture Benjamin hazarded towards the end of his essay. This is what "the Bilbao effect" means: the theatricalization of architecture at the expense of reducing the artistry of construction to the aesthetic of fetishism of commodity form. Purposely dismantled or unconsciously forgotten in parametric design is the structural organization system central to two concepts of frame promoted by Mies and Le Corbusier. In this advocacy for tectonic reconsideration, architecture loses its formal autonomy and becomes a fragment in the constellation of broader knowledge, the constructive principle of which is a montage.[97] Accordingly, without submitting to the exigencies of digital techniques, *construction*, as it concerns architecture, should open itself to the world, saving its claim on history while performing a critical role in the construction of the condition of life. It is indeed the task of committed architects to recognize the distinction between theatricalization, formal playfulness induced by digital techniques, and the theatricality central to Semper's notion of tectonics as elaborated in these pages.

I would like to finish this rather long recourse on technification with the following: Jacques Derrida writes, "Down even to its archaic foundation, the most fundamental concept of architecture has been *constructed*." He continues, "This naturalized architecture is bequeathed to us ... and we must recognize in it an *artefact*, a *construction*, a monument."[98] What one should make of his statement can be summed up this way: that architecture's production demands a conscious attempt on the part of the architect to engage with themes such as structure, space, and the tectonic earth-work and frame-work with consideration to the fact that "architecture has a history," and in association with the latest available technologies and the laws governing the organization of labor and construction techniques. In the age of digital reproducibility, what tectonics means to architecture is to make associations between the manifold consequences of the mechanical reproducibility of the artwork and the loss of aura. This involves a historical passage from poiesis to *techne*, establishing a critical dialogue between architecture and modernity. And yet, during the early decades of modernization, the reproduction of architecture was closer to *production*; whereas since the transformation from mechanical to digital reproducibility (the 1990s), architecture is conceived of as reproduction par excellence, a spectacular fabrication in the true sense of the word. Adorno had already anticipated this when he wrote, "If works become their own reproductions, the time when reproductions will become the works cannot be all that far away."[99] The dematerialization of architecture today, the reduction of its poiesis and many meaningful transformative (*Stoffwechsel*) interactions between various trades to image building, necessitates re-thinking Semper towards a constructive critique of the contemporaneity of architecture. A project that is centered on separating the art-form from the core-form, which is spatial with two connotations. Firstly, the enclosing wall has the least to do with the purpose of the space and is secondary to the symbolic surface articulations of the art-form. Accordingly, "solid walls are only an inner invisible scaffolding, hidden behind the true representative of the wall: the colored woven carpet."[100] Margaret Olin considers Semper, among others attracted to the British Arts and Crafts movement, as upholding the importance of the symbolic dimension of the work of art that during the early stages of the industrial revolution was degraded by machine products. Secondly, the Marxian dissociation between use value and exchange value was a familiar idea to the progressivist faction of the Arts and Crafts movement, and attained visibility as part of the experience of the Great Exhibition of 1851. While the distinction Semper made between the art-form and the core-form was part of his sympathy with Renaissance symbolic language, we must push the envelope further and plot it in association with the *image* already inscribed in the commodities paraded in the Crystal Palace. The dialectics between the image and the dematerialization implied in Semper's tectonics, I claim, is another reason for his relevance today when the commodity form prevails globally at the expense of the invisibility of the "falling rate of use value" in correspondence to the ascent of spectacle.[101]

In the remaining chapters of this book, I intend to take every opportunity to retrospectively historicize the spatial schism meaningful to Semper's theorization of tectonics towards a critique of the hyper-spectacle of digitally reproduced architecture. I am proposing a project of "resistance" that does not rely merely on the ingenuity of the architect but on his/her understanding of the semi-autonomous dynamics structuring the semiotic rectangle introduced in the introduction to this volume.

Notes

1 Marco Frascari, "The Tell-the-Tale Detail," *VIA*, no. 7 (1984): 23–37.
2 Gottfried Semper, *The Four Elements of Architecture and Other Writings*, Trans. Harry Francis Mallgrave & Wolfgang Hermann (Cambridge: Cambridge University Press, 1989).
3 Fredric Jameson, *The Benjamin Files* (London: Verso, 2020), 234.

4 Harry Harootunian, *The Unspoken as Heritage: The Armenian Genocide and Its Unaccounted Lives* (Durham: Duke University Press, 2019), 82.

5 See Murray Fraser, "Gottfried Semper and the Globalizing of the London Building World in the 1850s," in Michael Gnehm & Sonja Hildebrand, ed. *Architectural History and Globalized Knowledge: Gottfried Semper in London* (Zurich: gta Verlag, 2022), 15–37.

6 See Serge Guilbaut, *How New York Stole the Idea of Modern Art* (Chicago: The University of Chicago Press, 1983).

7 Facebook, checked in March 26, 2021. Bernard Cache, "Digital Semper," first posted at "boring classics," July 9, 2009.

8 Kenneth Frampton, *Studies in Tectonic Culture* (Cambridge: The MIT Press, 1995).

9 Isak Worre Foged & Marie Frier Havejsel, *Reader: Tectonics in Architecture* (Aalborg: Aalborg University Press, 2018).

10 Michael Gnehm & Sonja Hildebrand, ed. *Architectural History and Globalized Knowledge: Gottfried Semper in London* (Zurich: gta Verlag, 2022). And, Michael Gnehm, Sonja Hildebrand & Dieter Weidmann, ed. *Gottfried Semper: London Writings, 1850–1855* (Zurich: gta Verlag, 2022).

11 Gevork Hartoonian, *Ontology of Construction: On Nihilism of Technology in Theories of Modern Architecture* (Cambridge: Cambridge University Press, 1994).

12 Alina Payne, *From Ornament to Object: Genealogies of Architectural Modernism* (New Haven: Yale University Press, 2012).

13 Kenneth Frampton, *Modern Architecture: A Critical History* (London: Thames & Hudson, 1980), 34.

14 Douglas Murphy, *The Architecture of Failure* (London: Zero Books, 2012), 59.

15 Various aspects of which Susan Buck-Morss has eloquently unpacked in her, *The Dialectics of Seeing* (Cambridge: The MIT Press, 1989).

16 Quoted in Susan Buck-Morss, *The Dialectics of Seeing*, 1989, 111.

17 Quoted in Susan Buck-Morss, *The Dialectics of Seeing*, 1989, 114.

18 Alina Payne, "The Agency of Objects: From Semper to the Bauhaus and Beyond," in Ines Weizman, ed. *Dust & Data: Traces of the Bauhaus across 100 Years* (London: Spector Books, 2019), 24.

19 Jürgen Habermas, "Modernity—An Incomplete Project," in Hal Foster, ed. *The Antiaesthetic: Essays on Postmodern Culture* (Washington: Bay Press, 1983), 3–15.

20 Gottfried Semper, "London Lecture of November 11, 1853," *RES: Anthropology and Aesthetics*, no. 6 (Autumn 1983): 12.

21 I am benefiting from Fredric Jameson's reading of *Capital* at the expense of distorting his core argument. Jameson, *Presenting Capital: A Reading of Volume On* (London: Verso Books, 2011), 43.

22 Walter Benjamin, *The Arcades Project*, trans. H. Eiland & K. McLaughlin (Cambridge: Harvard University Press, 1999), 160. On this author's association between montage and tectonics, see Gevork Hartoonian, *Ontology of Construction*, 1994.

23 On this subject, see Gevork Hartoonian, *Architecture and Spectacle: A Critique* (London: Routledge, 2012).

24 Gottfried Semper, "London Lecture of November 11, 1853," *RES: Anthropology and Aesthetics*, no. 6 (Autumn 1983): 13.

25 William Haver, "Introduction," in Nishida Kitaro, trans. W. Haver, *Ontology of Production: 3 Essays* (Durham: Duke University Press, 2012), 20.

26 Joseph Rykwert, "London Lecture of November 11, 1853," *RES: Anthropology and Aesthetics*, no. 6 (Autumn 1983): 5–31.

27 Joseph Rykwert, *The Necessity of Artifice* (New York: Rizzoli International Publication Inc., 1982), 129.

28 Gottfried Semper, "London Lecture of November 11, 1853," *RES: Anthropology and Aesthetics*, no. 6 (Autumn 1983): 14.

29 See footnote 25, same page.

30 Again, with distortion, Fredric Jameson, *Presenting Capital*, 2011, 34.

31 Adolf Loos, *Ornament and Crime: Selected Essays* (California: Ariadne Press, 1998), 7.

32 Joseph Rykwert, "The Dark Side of the Bauhaus," in Michael Mitchell, trans. *The Necessity of Artifice*, 1982, 44–50.

33 Peter Stallybrass, "Marx's Coat," in Patricia Spyer, ed. *Border Fetishism: Material Object in Unstable Places* (London: Routledge, 1998), 183–207. Stallybrass makes an interesting association between Marx's discussion of a coat, a commodity form, with Marx's pawned coat, also elaborated in Alina Payne's essay noted above.

34 Adrian Forty, *Objects of Desire: Design and Society since 1750* (London: Thames & Hudson, 1986), 6.

35 See footnote 34.

36 Gevork Hartoonian, *Ontology of Construction*, 1994.

37 Gottfried Semper, "London Lecture of November 11, 1853," *RES: Anthropology and Aesthetics*, no. 6 (Autumn 1983): 12.

38 Walter Benjamin, *The Arcades Project*, 152.

39 Gottfried Semper, *Style in the Technical and Tectonic Arts; or, Practical Aesthetics*, introduction by Harry Francis Mallgrave (Los Angeles: The Getty Research Institute, 2004), 345. Semper's first statement is in italic in the English edition of the book and responds to Carl Botticher which I discuss in the next heading of this chapter.

40 Wolfgang Hermann, *Gottfried Semper: In Search of Style* (Cambridge: The MIT Press, 1978), 139–152.

41 On this subject, see Wolfgang Hermann, *Gottfried Semper*, 146–150. Also see Harry Francis Mallgrave, below footnote 44.

42 Gottfried Semper, *Style*, 2004, 238.

43 Harry Francis Mallgrave, *Gottfried Semper: Architect of the Nineteenth Century* (New Haven: Yale University Press, 1996), 219.

44 Harry Francis Mallgrave, *Gottfried Semper*, 1996, 220.

45 Wolfgang Hermann, *Gottfried Semper*, 147.

46 Joseph Rykwert, *The Dancing Column: On Order in Architecture* (Cambridge: The MIT Press, 1996), 7.

47 On Leon Battista Alberti, see Gevork Hartoonian, *Ontology of Construction*, 1994, chapter 1, 5–28.

48 Hubert Damisch, *Noah's Ark: Essays on Architecture* (Cambridge: The MIT Press, 2016), 70.

49 On this subject, see Wolfgang Hermann, *Gottfried Semper*, 146–150. Also see Harry Francis Mallgrave, *Gottfried Semper*,1996, 222.

50 Quoted in Wolfgang Hermann, *Gottfried Semper*, 1996, 147.

51 Kenneth Frampton, *Studies in Tectonic Culture* (Cambridge: The MIT Press, 1995).

52 Wolfgang Hermann, *Gottfried Semper*, 182.

53 Walter Benjamin, *The Arcades Project*, 1999, 150.

54 Harry Francis Mallgrave, "Introduction," in Otto Wagner, *Modern Architecture* (Los Angeles: The Getty Center Publication Program, 1988), 20.

55 Walter Benjamin, *The Arcades Project*, 1999, 157.

56 Gevork Hartoonian, from an unpublished manuscript.

57 On this subject, see Gevork Hartoonian, "Construction of the not yet Construed," in Ontology of Construction (Cambridge: Cambridge University Press, 1994), 81–90. Also see Marc-Antoine Laugier, An Essay on Architecture, trans. Wolfgang Hermann and Anni Herrmann (Los Angeles, Ingalls, 1977).

58 I am paraphrasing Hegel quoted in Hubert Damisch, *Noah's Ark: Essays on Architecture* (Cambridge: The MIT Press, 2016), 41. For a brief account of Hegel and other thinkers' account of orders, see Joseph Rykwert, *The Dancing Column*, 1996, 9–11.

59 Gevork Hartoonian, *Time, History and Architecture: Essays on Critical Historiography* (London: Routledge, 2019), 145.

60 On this subject, see Gevork Hartoonian, "Mies van der Rohe; the Genealogy of Column and Wall," *Journal of Architectural Education*, vol. 42, no. 2 (Winter 1989): 43–50.

61 Barry Bergdoll, *European Architecture 1750–1890* (Oxford: Oxford University Press, 2000), 24.

62 Antoine Picon, *The Materiality of Architecture* (Minneapolis: University of Minneapolis Press, 2020), 88.

63 Joseph Rykwert, *The Dancing Column*, 1996, 12.

64 Peter Stallybrass, "*Marx's Coat*," 1998, 189.

65 Both Hubert Damisch and Pier Vittorio Aurelie recognized the ordering role column plays in Alberti's architecture. See Hubert Damisch, *Noah's Ark*, 2016, 46–47. Pier Vittorio Aurelie, "Means to an End: The Rise and Fall of the Architectural Project of the City," in Aurelie, ed. *The City as a Project* (Berlin: Ruby Press, 2013), 26.

66 Hubert Damisch, *Noah's Ark*, 2016, 40.

67 Joseph Rykwert, *The Dancing Column*, 1996, 4.

68 The other two functional elements are attributed to the frame's capacity for "selection" and "connection." See Cache, "Architectural Image," in *Earth Moves: The Furnishing of Territories* (Cambridge: The MIT Press, 1995), 21–32.

69 I am benefiting and paraphrasing Joseph Rykwert's rhetorical techniques in advertising. See Rykwert, *Necessity of Artifice* (New York: Rizzoli International Publications, Inc, 1982), 59.

70 Walter Benjamin, *The Arcades Project*, 1999, 156.

71 I am benefiting from Jean-Louis Cohen's exhaustive introduction to *Toward an Architecture* (Los Angeles: The Getty Research Institute Publication Program, 2007), 1–82.

72 Kenneth Frampton, *Le Corbusier* (London: Thames and Hudson, 2001), 21.

73 Walter Benjamin, *The Arcades Project*, 1999, 155.

74 Le Corbusier, *Toward an Architecture*, 2007 (1924), 220.

75 See, for example, Hal Foster, "Go Modernity," *London Review of Books*, vol. 28, no. 12 (June 2006).

76 Martin Heidegger, *The Question Concerning Technology, and Other Essays* (New York: Harper Tourchbooks, 1977), 6–7.

77 Edmund Husserl's *Crisis of the European Sciences and Transcendental Philosophy*, published in Germany in 1936 and 1970 in English. For the reception of Husserl's taught in architecture, see Alberto Perez-Gomez, *Architecture and the Crisis of Modern Science* (Cambridge: The MIT Press, 1983).

78 William Haver, "Introduction," in Nishida Kitaro, trans. W. Haver, *Ontology of Production*, 2012, 5.

79 Fredric Jameson, *Representing Capital*, 2011, 102–103.

80 Theodor Adorno, *Aesthetic Theory* (London: Routledge & Kegan Paul, 1984), 32.

81 Theodor Adorno, *Sound Figures* (Stanford: Stanford University Press, 1994), 197–199.

82 Andrew Huyssen, "Adorno in Reverse: From Hollywood to Richard Wagner," *New German Critique*, no. 29 (Spring-Summer, 1983), 13.

83 Theodor Adorno, "Mediation," in *Introduction to the Sociology of Music* (New York: Continuum, 1989), 211.

84 Theodor Adorno, *Sound Figures* (Stanford: Stanford University Press, 1999), 202.

85 The subject was also discussed by Heinrich Wölfflin, Alois Riegl, and a number of other German scholars.

86 Walter Benjamin, *One-Way Street* (London: New Left Books, 1979), 250.

87 John Roberts, "Philosophizing the Everyday," *Radical Philosophy*, vol. 98 (November/December 1999), 20.

88 See the entire issue of *October*, vol. 35 (Winter 1985).

89 Quoted in Thomas Y. Levin, "Walter Benjamin and the Theory of Art History," *October* vol. 47 (Winter 1988): 80.

90 See Gevork Hartoonian, *Ontology of Construction*, 1994.

91 Walter Benjamin, "N [Re the Theory of Knowledge, Theory of Progress]," in Gary Smith, ed. *Benjamin: Philosophy, Aesthetics, History* (Chicago, IL: University of Chicago Press, 1989), 48.

92 I have taken up this subject in "Looking Backward, Looking Forward: Delightful Delays," in Gevork Hartoonian, ed. *Walter Benjamin and Architecture* (London: Routledge, 2010), 23–38.

93 Walter Benjamin, "The Work of Art in the Age of Mechanical Reproduction," in Hannah Arendt, ed. *Illuminations* (New York: Schocken Books, 1969), 239. Rosemarie Haag Bletter reminds us of Adolf Behne's discussion in *"Das reproduktive Zeitalter"* [The Reproductive Era] that prefigured Benjamin's thesis "about the effect of mass produced images on art." Arn Bohm first noted the association in an essay published in *The Germanic Review* vol. 68, no. 4 (1993): 146–155. See Haag Bletter, "Introduction" to Adolf Behne's *The Modern Functional Building* (Santa Monica, CA: The Getty Research Institute for History of Art and the Humanities, 1996), 5.

94 Walter Benjamin, "The Work of Art in the Age of Mechanical Reproduction" in *Illuminations*, trans. Harry Zohn (New York: Schocken Books, 1973), 217–252.

95 This aspect of the tectonic is indeed the theoretical underpinning of Gottfried Semper's theory of style. For a comprehensive understanding of Semper's theory of architecture, see Gottfried Semper, *Style in the Technical and Tectonic Arts; or Practical Aesthetics*, introduction by Harry Francis Mallgrave, trans. Harry Francis Mallgrave and Michael Robinson (Santa Monica, CA: Texts and Documents, The Getty Research Institute, 2004).

96 The distinction is essential for Kenneth Frampton's discourse in *Studies in Tectonic Culture* (Cambridge, MA: The MIT Press, 1995).

97 Here I am benefiting from Harry Harootunian in "The Benjamin Effect: Modernism, Repetition, and the Path to Different Cultural Imagination," in Michael P. Steinberg, ed. *Walter Benjamin and the Demands of History* (Ithaca: Cornell University Press, 1996), 62–87.

98 Jacques Derrida, "Point de folie—Maintenant l'architecture," *AA Files* no. 12 (Summer 1986): 65.

99 Theodor Adorno, *Sound Figures* (Stanford: Stanford University Press, 1994), 197–199.

100 Quoted in Margaret Olin, *Forms of Representation in Alois Riegl's Theory of Art* (University Park: The Pennsylvania University Press, 1992), 43.

101 Guy Debord, *Society of the Spectacle* (New York: Zone Books, 1994), 32.

2   On Materiality

The systematic industrial process, which converts the raw material into immediately available building material, begins with iron earlier than existing materials. Between matter and materials, in this case, there is a relationship quite different from that between stone and ashlar, clay and tile, timber and beam.

Walter Benjamin

Opening

Walter Benjamin's observation complements Gottfried Semper's anthropological investigation of how motives developed in industrial arts are transformed into style architecture. Matter plays an essential role in the implied biomorphic and transformative process (*Stoffwechsel*), and Semper attends to most pre-industrially processed materials except iron. Semper was aware of the use of iron in engineering and its contribution to erecting and covering large spanned spaces similar to the Crystal Palace designed by John Paxton. His minor engagement in the famous Great Exhibition, London (1851), including the arrangement of sections of a few countries,[1] allowed him to explore the Crystal Palace closely. However, his ambivalent position regarding the suitability of iron for monumental architecture had to do with iron's lack of "body" in contrast to traditional masonry materials used in the corner articulation of most classical buildings. And yet, Semper could not express his reservation about scientific development and the inauguration of new divisions of labor. Among other consequences, industrially reproduced materials tended to separate "the so-called ornamental from formal and technical aspects of art purely in a mechanical way betraying its lack of feeling for and misunderstanding of the true relationship between the various means the artist uses to produce his work."[2] More importantly, the industrially

DOI: 10.4324/9781003360445-3

produced materials with the related techniques further separated the already accepted division between the architect and the craft person as part of Leon Battista Albert's theorization of architecture.[3] The problem was not utterly innate to iron. It was part of Semper's belief that the world of architectural form does not arise solely "from structural and material conditions and that these alone supply the means for further development." For him, essential to the traditions of architecture were the historically developed motives produced by four industries; textiles, ceramics, carpentry, and masonry, each contributing the formal and artistic aspects of architecture. And most importantly, through *Stoffwechsel*, the material loses its deterministic role in the work's artistic *appearance*.

Throughout this chapter, I will argue that the notion of appearance connotes the image laminated to the masonry body of the language of classical architecture. This dimension of the preindustrial materials urged architects to conceive an appropriate "appearance" using industrially processed materials such as steel and glass during the first two decades of the last century. Benjamin's observation drew from the fact that in the mechanical reproducibility, the inherited means, and labor from the Arts and Craft tradition, the priority was given to materials and construction techniques congenial to the capitalistic production system. This was the founding idea behind the Deutsch Werkbund, Munich, Germany (1907), and the Bauhaus school, Weimar, Germany (1919). The importance Semper charged to *appearance* correlated to the experience of the commodity form, fashion, and photography. This dimension of Semper's work makes him relevant today when image-making and commodity form have taken over the cultural realm and architecture.

Accordingly, from the oldest to the most recent theorization of architecture, architects have given close attention to material and its transformation to materiality. This transformation involves two theoretical issues. Firstly, architecture should not be equated with construction, which reveals the physical and spatial outcome of the work carried out by various crafts and techniques in correspondence to the artistic image in the architect's mind delineated in drawings. There is, however, always an element of excess in architecture as materials are transformed into materiality by the agency of surface embellishment. This means that a material's natural attributes should be transformed into architectonic elements—formal or otherwise—that are culturally coded through and through. According to Semper, "when an artistic motive undergoes any kind of material treatment, its original type will be modified; it will receive, so to speak, a specific coloring. The type is no longer in its primary stage of development but has undergone a more or less pronounced metamorphosis."[4] Secondly, most architects start their design with an image in mind, about a *type* or *model*, if not a *form* with particular aesthetic connotations. This latter appropriation of the image, I will argue throughout this chapter, subdues materiality, endowing it with a "look" that has become the central aesthetic regime of digitally reproduced architecture today. Juxtaposing materiality with memory, Kenneth Frampton presents a critical reading of contemporary architecture's tendency to "aestheticize" materiality. He sees the loss of "containment" as an attribute of load-bearing masonry architecture due to the white architecture of the early modern movement and the glazed structures of the post-war era. He writes, "Irrespective of whether they happen to be used as cladding or as structural form, traditional materials such as brick, stone, and wood are cultural constructs" associable with a particular region.[5] Semper, on the other hand, highlighted the necessity to articulate the surface of material artistically, as a principle beyond regionalist metaphors that, according to classical treatises, were already transformed into the language of the Orders. However, as we noticed in the previous chapter, the different surface articulations of situa and hydria vessels corresponded to two different cultures evidence in their cultivation of land and lifestyle.

Highlighting the dialectics between perceptual lightness and heaviness, informing several selected contemporary buildings, this chapter will argue that "image" is inherent in architecture. However, its mode of appropriation has radically changed since Benjamin formulated the loss of aura. Following Benjamin, and at the expense of simplifying his discourse, we might say that the aura recalls a historical situation when the technique was integral to the processes of thinking and making. The latter's scope of transformation was essential to the craftsperson's knowledge of the symbolic purpose of the produced object.[6] The intention is not to repudiate Semper's take on the subject but to stress the need for a critical assessment of materiality in contemporary architecture. To this end, I will map the historicity of image and materiality, as evidenced in several relevant architectural treatises. Particular attention will be given to Semper's formulation of tectonic theatricality as a functional theoretical paradigm for addressing materiality in architecture.

In contemporary literature, the idea of the image is most often considered in conjunction with discussions focused on technology. Following the invention of film and photography, Benjamin suggested that our perception of the phenomenal world changes along with humanity's experience of temporality. He wrote, "Since the historical testimony rests on the authenticity, the former, too, is jeopardized by reproduction when substantive duration ceases to matter." Benjamin concluded that "for the first time in world history, mechanical reproduction emancipates the work of art from its parasitical dependence on ritual."[7] Accordingly, before the advent of mechanical reproduction, architecture was experienced and understood concerning broader associations as symbolic and metaphorical interpretations of heavenly and earthly domains. In pre-modern times, material mattered for its color, softness, or hardness, and how these *natural* qualities had to be respected and worked towards the realization of forms and objects that, in return, would evoke these same natural attributes. This was also a time when, in addition to the material itself, the laws of mechanics were considered to be embedded in Nature, the operative domain of which was understood in the metaphysics of Christianity. Giulio C. Argan, for one, sees the entire edifices of the classical theory of mimesis as based on the belief that technology is "*a priori* in the natural world created by God."[8] Still, in pre-modern times, the word *techne* suggested that technique itself was valued for its association with the artistic articulation of material and form. This perceived unity between technique, material, and the *work* was reincarnated during the industrial revolution through a nostalgic recollection of the artisanal authorship of design, including those processes involved in the choice of material and technique. I use the word "work" in italic to recall Frampton's distinction between labor and work, as discussed by Hannah Arendt.[9] As for the *fabrication*, which brings together labor, material, and technique, Arendt wrote:

> The actual work of fabrication is performed under the guidance with which the object is constructed. This model can be an image beheld by the mind's eye or a blueprint in which the image has already found a tentative materialization through work. In either case, what guides the work of fabrication is outside the fabricator and precedes the actual work process in much the same way as the urgencies of the life process within the laborer precede the actual labor process.[10]

For Frampton, such a model is a "cultural construct," an attribute of work that holds together craft and the rationale of intentionality implied in the article cited earlier. As we will notice towards the end of this essay, the title of Frampton's essay recalls Auguste Perret's position on concrete materiality. Cut between Renaissance and

Gothic tectonic traditions, Perret presented a far-advanced interpretation of the latter's artistic style. Contrary to the romantic advocates of the Arts and Crafts, the French architect avoided reducing "artistic appearance" (Semper) to the material. As for the materiality of concrete, it is essential to recognize the subjectivity emulating concrete during early modernism from postwar and contemporary architecture. For one, the concrete used in most of Zaha Hadid's early projects are animated and less sculptural than the post-war brutalist architecture.[11] Whereas Perret's and even Le Corbusier's emulation of concrete was part of modernism's tendency to explore the architectonics of various materials, the architecture of brutalism should be associated with the post-war "experience of poverty," actual and phenomenal. In consideration of the use of concrete in Brazilian architecture, Adrian Forty writes that the ideological content of European brutalism "brings with it a cargo of irrationalism, where architectonic form, despite its appearance of technical determinism, was arrived at through arbitrary or accidental aesthetic choices." He proclaims that "European Brutalism was an expression of melancholy, the work of a civilization that had all but destroyed itself in the Second World War, and whose use of technology was always now tainted by knowledge of its own capacity for self-destructiveness."[12] Forty's position recalls Benjamin's 1933 essay where he associates the poverty of humanity with the development of technology, hence a new kind of barbarism. The current turn to digital reproducibility instead extends the impoverished animated figure of Mickey Mouse to architecture.[13] The animation of the naked body of concrete in contemporary architecture alludes to the abstraction involved in the experience of subjectivity with the Real, wherein aesthetics of the commodity form fully conquers the image of reality.

Truth to the Material!

A modern classical disposition of the artisanal belief in "truth to material" is delivered in John Ruskin's *The Seven Lamps of Truth* (1848). He presents four sources of architectural deceits, two of which had a lasting influence on architecture. These two are one-structural deceit, using structural elements that have nothing to do with the load and support system of the building. Two-surface deceit; painting a material contrary to its natural color.[14] Ruskin's importance to the Arts and Craft movement,[15] and the formation of the early modern architecture needs no emphasis here. What should be highlighted is Ruskin's romantic—if not religious—indulgence with design as the direct result of the labor of hand, one consequence of which was to negate the artistry, the subjective involved in the transition of material into materiality. He considered materiality a moralistic interpretation of truth in the material. Criticizing the use of marble in early Venetian Renaissance buildings, Ruskin asked what advantages would have followed if marble were used as "Nature would have us."[16] Interestingly enough, his exposition, the idea that material should be used following its natural attributes (matter?), was challenged by Owen Jones. In *The Grammar of Ornament* (1856), he suggested that truth to the material was about the appearance of truth.[17] The purpose of ornamentation was indeed to dematerialize the material. Ruskin pronounced his idea at a time when, having an eye on the developmental processes of capitalism, Karl Marx had claimed that everything solid, including the truth to material, would melt into air. I am paraphrasing Marx in *Communist Manifesto*, proclaiming, "All that is solid melts into air, and all that is holy profaned, and man is at last compelled to face with sober senses his real condition of life, and his relations with his kind."[18] Sympathetic to the Ruskinian view of how natural elements "furnish" each other, Lars Spuybroke writes that "Things only start to network when they have exceeded their use value, turning them into acts of pure care."[19] We will look into his interpretation of the Gothic tectonics. For now and regarding his own take on digital architecture, it is enough to say that Marx's dictum is relevant to today's virtual state of floating and unbounded objects, architecture remains a bastion of resistance against technological nihilism. Unlike most commodities, architecture is not moveable. It stands firm and stable even if it might look otherwise in most digitally reproduced buildings.

It took humanity another century to experience the nihilism implied in Marx's statement in many fields. I am reminded of Milan Kundera's novel, *The Unbearable Lightness of Being* (1984). Italo Calvino's *Six Memos of the Next Millennium* (1985), where one of the memos underlines the importance of the notion of lightness.[20] It is this perception of lightness, I posit, that has become the main occupation of architectural experience in the present age of digital reproducibility. To establish this claim, it is helpful to remember that there is always an image at work in architecture that, one way or another, is imbued with materiality; and that the idea of lightness as delivered by nineteenth-century steel and glass structures and its aestheticization in the work of Renzo Piano and Norman Foster today, should be differentiated from the lightness implied in Zaha Hadid's architecture, to mention a practice that exploits parametric techniques to its extreme. The difference is one reason why Hal Foster characterized the work of Renzo Piano and Norman Foster as "late modern." Accordingly, the British architect approximates the state of the early modern architecture, the white, abstract, and rectilinear variety of Adolf Loos and Le Corbusier, while capturing the contemporary look. Such architecture "still appears modern when almost nothing else of the period does make the cars, the clothes, or the people."[21] Exploring the glass architecture of post-Mitterrand Paris, Annette Fierro distinguishes between modernist "technological rhetoric" and the political incentives of most buildings covered with surface transparencies. She writes, in Foundation Cartier, Jean Nouvel "insisted that material, or matter, might be called upon to record the city as filmic experience. The material thus enfolds and subsumes the incorporation of event."[22] Should we separate the light structures built during the last century from the "pervasive political and social agenda centered on the desire to free humanity from the unnecessary burden of an industrial age now perceived as antiquated."[23] With its visually charged theatricality, Hadid's early sculpted tectonics, further elaborated below, subdues the material qualities of concrete, revealing a different sense of lightness. The playfulness of digital architecture also differs from the early modern expressionism, which was not solely driven by technique as is the case with the former. Introducing the notion of *economy of material* in the coda of this essay, I will present two examples of contemporary architecture where, in addition to lightness, the image operates in both cases as a political agency, resisting the tendency for local identity the architectonics of the global spectacle.

Material of History: Alberti, Ruskin

In a structuralist reading of Viollet-le-Duc's discourse, Hubert Damisch wrote that the French architect's analysis visualizes the differences between form and construction, analogous to the relationship between an architectural whole and its parts. Accordingly, rather than the reality of the stones and mortar used in Gothic architecture (Ruskin's position), Viollet-le-Duc saw in cathedrals a model in the structuralist sense of the term. Damisch notes, "The visible framework, the tracery of ribbing and salient features which are thrown over masonry like a net, immediately suggests to the observer a structuralist scheme which certainly does not correspond to a theory of construction." For the French architect, the truth of architecture rested neither in the empirical reality of material (matter?) nor its compositional form, but somewhere between form and substance, architecture and construction, where image and materiality are fused.[24]

More recently, Antone Picon has suggested that for Viollet-le-Duc Gothic architecture "was as much a system of rationales as it was a set of spatial devices and constructional techniques based on pointed arches, slender pillars, and flying buttresses."[25] Tracing the schism between form and construction in Leon Battista Alberti's theorization of architecture, Mario Carpo has also written that *Linamenta* suggested an image of the work, generated in advance and independent of construction. During the Renaissance, architecture was perceived through a complete set of drawings and models that preceded construction. The identity between building and conceiving was, according to Carpo, sustained through notations, including those concerned with materiality.[26] Without pursuing the implications of materiality for architecture, Carpo presents the algorithms of digitally reproduced architecture as the third stage in the Humanist history of design, after the artisanal authorship (Brunelleschi) followed by the intellectual or notational authorship (Alberti). Carpo leaves the political economy of digital architecture unnoticed. For example, the digital authorship of Frank Gehry's design for the Walt Disney Concert Hall[27] was initially rejected by construction industries because it was unbuildable with traditional methods. When the drawings were almost completed, the team realized that Disney's animated products is one thing; in architecture, "images require tectonics."[28] Making "alliances between organic inspiration and the use of algorithms," Picon writes, digital culture "is likely revealing a form of nostalgia that is linked to the sense that it is difficult to repair the rift between information designers manipulate and the matter to which applied."[29] Taking into consideration the above-mentioned authors' reflections on aspects of materiality, what I wish to map in this chapter is the suggested rift in analogy to the distinction Semper made between the tectonic of theatricality and theatricalization.

In the hierarchy underpinning the organization of *De re aedificatoria*, Alberti squeezed his manuscript to cover the subject of material between two books, each addressing issues such as *lineaments* and *construction*. The word *material* is mentioned for the first time in the fourth passage of the second book, highlighting the importance of representational issues such as drawings and model making and those related to construction, for example, labor cost, etc. In all these, Alberti prioritized the body and nature to the point that the examination of the model of a building was valued about what he called "human capacity," meaning that nothing should be undertaken that "might immediately come into conflict with Nature."[30]

Alberti rationalized his reflection on the natural origin of material as if architectural conventions were cohered into the existential domain of humanity. He believed an elegant and perfect construction is achievable when it confirms his association between materials and one or more of the four seasons. Not all architects followed his logic: Filarete established a different rapport between materials and architectonic elements. He associated the wall with *signoria* (governing authority) and the bricks with the people.[31] The alleged division would stand firm when bricks are orderly lined up to support the gravity forces. Alberti's interpretation also focused on the skilled artisans at the construction site. As for materiality, he wrote, it was the task of the architect to demonstrate a comprehensive knowledge of the classical orders and their formal dispositions as documented through notations.[32] In any event, by 1900, the brick attained a new metaphoric dimension; its solidity was taken for the conspiratorial history of the workers' movement and the emergence of the brigades.[33]

As for material and its transformation to materiality, the difference between Ruskin and Alberti is notable. In the nineteenth-century revivalist environment, what seemed "natural" to Ruskin was an image of a cathedral sustaining the presumed literal transparency between materiality and construction. Scorning the Venetian use of marble, Ruskin wrote, "… so far as the desirableness of this or that method of ornamentation is to be measured by the fact of its simple honesty or dishonesty, there is little need to add anything to what has been already urged upon the subject."[34] This was about the ideas discussed in *The Seven Lamps of Architecture*. Accordingly, the architecture image was perfectly harmonious with the constructed form if the earlier mentioned four deceits, structural, aesthetic, surface, and what he called operative, were successfully avoided. In the same manuscript, he over-values human labor, saying that the correct question concerning ornament is not about the material but "was it done by enjoyment? Was the carver happy while he was doing it?[35] Ruskin wished to establish transparency between craft-person, labor, and material to roll back Alberti's designation of authorship to the architect. During the early Humanist architecture, labor had not attained *visibility* to make a distinctive factor in Ruskinian aesthetics. As we will see shortly below, Ruskin's ideas were taken to a new level in Le Corbusier's later work.[36]

Putting Alberti side by side with Ruskin, the intention is to demonstrate how the image is domesticated in their contrasting architectural theories. Alberti's text promotes an image where the conventions of the classical language of architecture are presented as *natural* and in organic rapport with architecture. Ruskin's proclamation instead is based on the belief that the natural *is the genesis* of architecture, an idea also shared by Spuybroek, mentioned earlier. In Ruskin's words, the value of architecture depends on "the image it bears of the natural creation." He wrote that architecture is "a noble rendering of images of Beauty, derived chiefly from the external appearances of organic nature."[37] As for Alberti, architecture was part of the Humanist culture, an artifact conceived independently of both nature and the legacies of Gothic architecture. Ruskin was interested in Gothic because it demonstrated "a continuity of elements and discontinuity of bodies" as biological evidence.[38] Helpful for this discussion is Semper's characterization of Renaissance and Gothic architecture; one incomplete and open to re-interpretation, the other complete in its distinction between the support and infill elements.[39]

Material of History: Semper

In contrast to his contemporary historicists and futurists, Semper argued that what governs architecture are transformative principles borrowed from four technical arts mentioned earlier. What transformative meant to him was that whereas the early correctness in technical skills was "to be a *natural and logical consequence of the raw material,*"[40] in the case of architecture, the borrowed motives transcend their original raw quality, attaining different visibility in correspondence to the phenomenal world, to use a Semperian terminology. Semper plotted the four early technical arts in parallel to four raw materials listed as pliable (brutal), soft (malleable), stick-shaped (elastic), and strong (densely aggregated), respectively. Even though his architecture was in continuation of the linguistic potentialities of the Renaissance, Semper's theory offers a hiatus for the imagination to breathe anew. Consider this: the architectural image delivered through Alberti's discourse was part of the emerging culture of Humanism and the tendency to see and totalize architecture as a simulation of the Divine forces. Ruskin's notion of the image, on the other hand, was part of the Romanticists' reaction against the nihilism of technology and the bourgeoisie's re-structuralization of the scope of temporality across the cultural aspects of modern everyday life.

Interestingly enough, Semper shared similar views with Ruskin on many issues directly related to the impact of modernization on the artwork. For example, both agreed that architecture is not just construction and that the balance of aesthetics was turning, slowly but surely, in favor of sight and vision at the expense of other senses. On the opening page of "The Lamp of Sacrifice," Ruskin wrote, "Architecture is the art which so disposes and adorns the edifices raised by man, for whatsoever uses, that the sight of them may contribute to his mental health, power, and pleasure." He added that "It is very necessary, at the outset of all inquiry, to distinguish carefully between architecture and building."[41] The distinction is also central to Semper's theory of architecture. On several occasions in *Der Stil*, Semper explains how difficult it is to hold on to the traditions of Humanism in architecture. He was at pain, Harry Francis Mallgrave reminds us, "to point out that by 'material' he meant both the physical matter and the theme or content of the work of art,"[42] or materiality as discussed through these pages. At the same time, Semper extended his criticism of the rising market economy to "speculative aesthetics." He wrote:

> This aesthetics lacks a concrete understanding of beauty. It may have generated much artistic rhetoric but minor artistic sensitivity. It has not found the source of formal beauty; as a role, it has to be content with distilling only the abstract spirit of the idea from the full grape. Speculative aesthetics finds its support in the inability of so many people to find pure enjoyment in beauty as such.[43]

Semper's reflection on speculative aesthetics concerned philosophy applied to art which often attempts to solve a philosophical problem with the least commonality with the artist whose work draws from the phenomenal world. Instead, "the appreciation of art is an intellectual exercise or a philosophical delight for the aesthetician."[44] However, by 1869, Semper noted that the stone-related architecture of plastic and iconographic expressions had become "antiquated in the face of new social and fiscal constraints as well as the pace of technological change." This awareness, which also alludes to his work in Dresden, was part of the conviction that at one point in time, architects would "shake contemporary design loose from trammels of the past."[45] Until that time arrives, Semper wrote, "we must reconcile ourselves to do as best we can with the old."[46] This much is evident in the Zurich Polytechnikum (designed in collaboration with Johann Caspar Wolf), the building's three-tier surface articulation sustains the notion of frontality in contradistinction with the rear façade. Whereas in the tradition of the Florentine Renaissance palaces, rustication cladding is chosen for the entry level of both sides of the building, the entry cladding of the upper two tiers enjoys rich "sgraffito decoration" in contrast to the rear façade's plain punctuated by window openings.[47]

Compared to Ruskin and Alberti's theories, the duality inform-ing Semper's tectonics, the core-form (*Kernform*) and the art-form

(*Kunstform*), is structural-symbolic rather than structural-technical. Thus, the art-form is not an aesthetic form independent of the transformation of material into materiality. Making a distinction between matter and material and criticizing the materialist reliance on structure and material conditions, Semper argued that "The material is subservient to the idea and is by no means the *only* factor controlling the idea's physical manifestation in the phenomenal world." He continued, "Although form—the idea made visible—should not conflict with the material out of which it is made, it is not absolutely necessary for the material *as such* to be a factor in artistic appearance."[48] Accordingly, we should agree with Alina Payne that Semper's theory of architecture was overwhelmingly progressive concerning the nineteenth century's broad interest in constructing a "culture of objects."[49] Attending the same subject on a different occasion, Payne writes that Semper's "was not nostalgic William Morris-like concern, but rather a concern that the evacuation of making from the production of objects broke the chain of layered meanings of materials succeeding each other in time (of the continuous *stoffwechsel*) and therefore also meant the evacuation of meaning *tout court*."[50] We cannot but agree with her conclusion that the dematerialization of object pertinent to digital reproducibility awaits serious attention. To this end, the four essays collected in this book provide the themes essential for the critique of the contemporaneity of architecture.

In the second volume of *Der Stil* (1860–63), Semper takes up a range of materials discussing each in "aesthetic-formal" and "technical-historical" categories. This chapter has no room for a detailed discussion of *Der Stil*'s second volume, which compromises almost more than half of the book. However, relevant to the subjects thus far explored, it is helpful to recall several points briefly shedding light on Semper's unique position on materiality in architecture and its implications for moveable objects, utensils, and furnishers the motifs of which are transferred to architecture. For example, he makes an analogical comparison between the stand upright kettles and those hang-down-like tubes and the vertical wall curtains.[51] Further interest to this book is the principle of tectonics wherein the matter, stone, is transformed in consideration to the phenomenal world, according to which the formal "will be most satisfying to the eye" without evoking material and duration, "much less raises doubt about either."[52] This is the case with the rusticated ashlar, the two-part surface articulation of the edge and its face that "concerns with the economy and solidity" and aesthetics. For Semper, "an ashlar block with raised face expresses resistance more clearly than a *smooth* one"[53] (Figure 2.1).

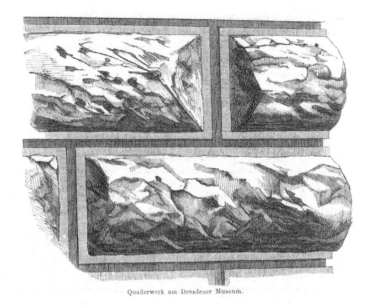

Quaderwerk am Dresdener Museum.

Figure 2.1 Ashlar, Gottfried Semper, Der Stil, 1860.

Source: Image courtesy of Getty Research Institute, Los Angeles.

Accordingly, we could suggest that the red-brick wall in Louis I. Kahn and Alvar Aalto's work would have remained for Semper a structural-technical solution if it had not been emancipated from the wall's urform, turning the foundational support into an artistic representation of their load-bearing function. A case in point is Mies van der Rohe's re-coding of the brick wall in Wolf House, Gubin (1925–27). The building's window opening of the living room exceeds the expected correspondence between load and support, introducing excess aesthetics beyond Semper's anticipation or expectation! Mies was also reversing Kahn's hypothetical dialogue with the brick wall, saying that "you" will look aesthetically pleasing with a concrete lintel instead of an arch.

For Semper, architecture's meaning is suggested in transforming construction into the cultural realm, that is, the language of monumentality and ornamentation. He wrote that whether a vessel is made for *containing, scooping,* or *filling,* what makes it belong to the cultural realm of objects (*Sachkultur*) is the vessel's surface articulation. In the original manuscript, he claimed that "a transition from timber construction to column architecture proper would not have been possible without an intermediate stage. The timber style must have been modified by a prior change in material and could have evolved from this change to stone style only through the mediation of the second change in material."[54] What *mediation* means here relates to the exchange of material motives, *Stoffwechsel*, already at work in decorative arts whose craft, purpose, and materiality had the least to do with architecture. Semper saw an artistic connection between the image of architecture and construction material and techniques employed. He also highlighted the aesthetic of theatricality for architecture's visibility within the cultural domain. This is important because tectonics relates to construction analogically.

Carl Bötticher is the German architect who initially discussed tectonics' theatrical and animated dimensions. Influenced by Arthur Schopenhauer's theorization of the animate state of force and support in architecture, Bötticher presented the dialectics suggestively associating the constructed form with its symbolic expression (the art-form). However, according to Mallgrave, he strove to demonstrate that "the decorative parts of the Greek temple emanated from or were closely connected with construction."[55] In any event, Semper came across Bötticher's book *Die Tektonic der Hellenen* (1844–52) in the British Museum in 1852. Impressed by the text, he gave a twist to the animism implied in the duality between the core-form and the art-form, along with his style theory. Semper re-coded the Renaissance three-part compositional principle from the simplistic observation that weight and heaviness must be represented as support. He wrote that the "rusticated ashlar resulted not only from concerns with economy and solidity but also from aesthetic considerations that more or less became conscious." In the same page, as we noted earlier, Semper recognizes two formal elements in ashlar; "the edge and the face." The latter "is framed; the former is the frame."[56] The distinction should be associated with the early nineteenth-century frame and infill structures. However, Semper was interested in highlighting the expression of resistance even though he recognized the frame-infill in the Caribbean huts displayed in the Crystal Palace, 1851. Either way, what interests us is the face of ashlar used in the Dresden Museum; its heavy and load-bearing part is decorative, alluding to the natural state of the stone, whereas the so-to-speak frame is "active inwardly." The animistic articulation of the ashlar's face speaks for the implied notion of theatricality in Semper's tectonics, knowing that excess has the least to do with the supportive function of a loadbearing element; it instead directs the spectator's attention to the building's artistic/aesthetic dimension. Here a distinction should be made between the inevitable rapport between an art object and the viewer from the commodities' affiliative connection with the spectator uniquely experienced in the interior atmosphere of the Crystal Palace. What Semper pursued in his design (arrangement) of the Canadian compartment was to demonstrate how a product is developed out of the gradual transformation of material, techniques, and skills.[57] In a page-long footnote to the "textiles" section of his book, Semper further suggests that "The destruction of reality, of the material, is necessary if the form is to emerge as a meaningful symbol, as an autonomous human creation." He does not support "speculative aesthetics" but highlights the deep historical origins of architecture's artistic motives.[58]

For a better understanding of architecture's artistic historicity, we should turn to the idea of *Stoffwechsel* one more time. Literary meaning metabolism, *Stoffwechsel* connotes a complicated sense of appropriation, a metabolic production process. Meaning that a genetic and transformative cord relates the early symbolic properties to its later and more advanced articulations. Also, "the resulting new form will be a composite, one that expresses the primeval type and all the stages preceding the latest form."[59] And yet, a nation's "growing sensitivity to beauty is inextricably bound up with true progress and the flourishing of industry in general, even in material respects," writes Semper.[60] Even Caesar Augustus' Ara Pacis altar, writes Akos Moravanaszky, "was much more than a place for sacrificial rites because it was also designed to ensure that the reason for its construction remained in the collective memory. Hence the decoration of the marble wall between the altar and the temple imitated the wooden planks, decorated with garlands of flowers, which screened off the scared space."[61] The altar thus signified its meaningfulness in two ways, as a monument reminding the society of an event and as an artifact recalling the material and technical metamorphosis of a wooden fence. Still, suppose we follow Semper's proclamation that textiles and weaving represent the ur-form of technical arts. In that case, the modernist distinction between frame and infill draws from, in addition to ashlar mentioned earlier, the technical aesthetics informing the production and appropriation of Assyrian carpet and Egyptian latticework later to be emulated in the Roman stone floor tiles. In the latter, but also similar to Assyrian doors, the main figurative surface is framed by a border with a different weaving pattern. Henry Sullivan's the Framers' National Bank comes to mind as a case representing the transformative modification of Semper's theorization of the surface from carpet and weaving to a brick wall. The brick wall in Sullivan's building has the least to do with the brick as material and matter. Instead, the brick has attained a different technical aesthetics as part of the material transformation (brick) to materiality. Sullivan's building confirms the Semperian claim that "artistic motive is carried through successive materials and methods of treatment."[62] In passing, we should notice the centrality of the concept of *Stoffwechsel* in Semper's progressive development from embossed hollow metal sculpture to Hellenic marble sculpture and its relevance for the realization of the capital used in Persepolis. Even though, Semper reminds us that architecture "went through a significantly greater number of material metamorphoses than sculpture," should not we make an association between the hollow metal sculpture and Kahn's use of the "hollow column" in the Trenton Bath House, New Jersey (1954) and the architect's proposal for a welded tubular steel structure project for Philadelphia most likely influenced by Robert Le Ricolais' experimental work.[63]

Now, if Alberti legitimized the authorship of the architect independent of the artisanship involved in the construction site, and despite Ruskin's attempt to reunite the craft of building with the art of design, Semper correctly underlined the technical nature of the transformation of material to materiality. Even though architectural production should recognize the autonomous and general course of technological inventions, the modification, the change of material to the applicability, was for Semper carried out by architectural techniques in the first place. Herein lies the primacy of the principle of cladding and the *lawful articulation* of "surface"; not the actual surface of the raw material, but the material that has been prepared (the constructed form) to receive linear or planar motifs, the ontology of which goes back to the textiles. It took architects a long time to modify the steel used in railroads and other engineering products such that it could be part of modernist steel and glass architecture, Mies's Seagram Building in Manhattan, for one.

As noted previously, Semper had reservations concerning iron structure dissimilar to Ruskin's negative remarks on this industrially produced material. For Semper, iron was unsuitable for monumentality because the latter's aesthetics (image) was traditionally comprehended through masonry materials such as brick and marble. The lightness permeating Joseph Paxton's Crystal Palace challenged the perception of heaviness essential to classical architecture. Thus, the criticality of the notion of *Stoffwechsel*, the idea that motifs transformed from textiles and carpentry to architecture operated in the tectonic as image-form. One implication of this proposition is to recognize the Semperian notion of semi-autonomy with this connotation: the work should establish an immanent relationship between purpose, material/technique, and the actualization of what he called the structural-symbolic dimension of the tectonic theatricality.[64] More important is Semper's tectonic mediation between the technical and cultural gap. This is important not only because the project of modernity was primarily concerned with the re-activation of the crisis of the object but also because in the age of digital reproducibility, the culture is focused on "image building," the aesthetic of which is experienced independently of material.

Sculpted Tectonics

Two things bring together the projects discussed in this section. Firstly, most of Zaha Hadid's early projects can be associated with Robin Evans's characterization of *trompes* and stone cuts, delivering a perception of lightness.[65] Secondly, Hadid's use of two-dimensional painterly diagrams has aesthetic connotations beyond what can be achieved by employing the Corbusian Dom-ino frame. In addition to the Semperian idea of theatricality, these projects also represent a benchmark in the architect's turn to digital techniques and synthetic materials. These differences confirm Semper's prediction that scientific and technological innovations will have a particular impact on the artistic and technical dimension of architecture in capitalism. Modern construction materials and techniques had problematized the continuity of traditional architectonics, allowing Semper to associate building motives with four artistic techniques. Even though I have discussed these works on another occasion, I chose to include them here because they stand at the threshold of the firm's turn to fully using digital design techniques and employing images associable with a blob or undulating topographic forms.[66]

According to Evan, trompes were conceived as structures in their own right, facilitating additions to an existing building. It was built out of drawings called *traits,* where the geometric matrix of lines defines the stereotomic nature of the surface. The implied "shape" dictates the cuts to be made in the various pieces of stone used in the *trompes.* Evans's investigation highlights the perceptual contrast between the lightness delivered in projective geometry and the heaviness of stones depicted in *traits.* Accordingly, it's not far-fetched to say that a similar difference informs "image" in contemporary architecture; Zaha Hadid's early work is a good case to differentiate her work from post-war brutalism. In the Vitra Fire Station (1990–94) and Leone/Landesgarten Schau (1996–99) (Figure 2.2), two works from her early

Figure 2.2 Zaha Hadid, Leone/Landesgarten Schau, Weil am Rhein, Germany, 1996–99 (general view).

Source: Photograph courtesy of Helen Binet, London.

portfolio, the image is meticulously woven with concrete materiality. While both projects animate the aesthetic of brutalism, the design stops short of entertaining the biomorphic surfaces that permeate the firm's latest work. Even though historical examples of poured-in-concrete construction did not wholly meet Viollet-le-Duc's "expectations regarding the 'truth' of the structure," their tectonic expression, according to Jean-Louis Cohen, did herald the Semperian dialectics between the core-form and the art-form.[67] To put it differently, what the texture of the formwork leaves on the surface of the concrete is "generated by the automatism of construction."[68] In the same line of consideration, reflecting on Le Corbusier's La Tourette, Hubert Damisch wrote, "the constructive aspects was translated by a kind of overflowing of the substance the building made of: the cement pouring vie with the many traces of a transubstantiation that in places takes on a quasi-pictorial quality."[69] Central to these observations is the expressive dimension of construction's relation to material, which is not pre-imagined.

In the Vitra, the perception of lightness is further extenuated by the metal screen grilles and the shape of the window cuts. These and the cuts implemented in the building's massing reveal tectonic figuration that concerns movement and theatricality at the expense of construction material. The perception of lightness delivered in Hadid's project also differs from the ethereal quality of Le Corbusier's Ronchamp Chapel, where the whitewash cladding of walls has an "equivocal nature" and gives them weightlessness and "appearance of *papier-mache.*"[70] According to Hadid, the firm's latest projects benefit from Frei Otto, "who achieved the most elegant designs based on material-structural form-finding processes. We learned from Frei Otto how the richness, organic coherence, and fluidity of the forms and spaces we desire could emerge rationally from an intricate balance of forces. We expanded Frei Otto's method to include environmental and structural logics, and we moved from material to computational simulations."[71] This consideration marks the beginning of biomorphic form in her work, coinciding with the rapid dissemination of the aesthetics of commodity form across the cultural realm, from videos to films and architecture. These projects suggest two things: Firstly, the transformation from construction to architecture is simultaneously welded to the change of material to materiality. Secondly, Hadid's understanding of materiality is not limited to the nature of the material but includes design strategies aimed at juxtaposing stability with the expression of animation.

In analogy to *trompes*, the *surface gauches* in Hadid's architecture attempt to defy the forces of gravity and the matter of materiality. However, in most cases in the firm's later work, the image of lightness (the look) precedes both materiality and the shape of cuts. Furthermore, these cuts turn the entire edifice into an ornament, placing the work on the borderline between the aesthetics of spectacle permeating today's culture and the Semperian tectonic of theatricality. Call it the "social construction of technology," the aesthetic theatricality turns the heavy feeling of the concrete mass into an agent of lightness.[72] The lesson we should draw from these observations involves the metamorphosis of the heavy mass of concrete to look as light as a feather, bringing forth several dichotomies essential for the transformational processes and versatility of industrially processed building materials.

Coda

For Semper, *excess in architecture* alludes to the gap informing the tectonic, the dialogue between the art-form and core-form discussed in the previous chapter. The "informing" here does not operate in a deterministic way. The Semperian art-form does not mirror the core-form, that is, construction; their complex rapport goes like this: "Sure, the picture is in my eye, but I am also in the picture."[73] Accordingly, *excess* in Hadid's work, as presented here, intermingles the image with the construction material. However, the constructive logic central to tectonics might, paradoxically, deconstruct both the positivistic and moralistic interpretations of material and technique. The impact of technology on architecture mediates through aesthetics— that is, by the expected artistic and cultural transformation of material to materiality. The image does not vanish; its metaphorical transformation is locked into construction. And yet, the image permeating contemporary architecture differs from that of the Renaissance and the architecture of the New Brutalism. As a precursor to Hadid's sculpted tectonics, Brutalism's architectural image is informed by the fusion of aesthetics with the ethical, to recall Ruskin.

Throughout this chapter, the ethical and aesthetic difference has been considered helpful in pitting Alberti against Ruskin. The following dialectical counterpoise to this conceptual pairing is essential for understanding the genetic difference between post-war Brutalism and Hadid's early sculpted tectonics. Her occasional turn to polished, sculpted, and organic forms warrant a departure from the materiality and detailing detectable in her work discussed earlier. On the one hand, this departure should be contextualized in the historicity of Russian Constructivism, a movement that undeniably has been inspirational till her recent turn to Frei Otto. On the other hand, Zaha Hadid's current projects should be contextualized along with two approaches to materiality evident in Vladimir Tatlin's "corner relief" and Naum Gabo's sculptures, two protagonists of objectivity in constructivism. Tatlin's corner reliefs are montages of unrefined raw materials such as iron, wood, and metal rods. Gabo also pursued similar techniques of montage, with the exception that he charged the final work with a polished look, the origin of which had to do with purist aesthetics. This comparative pairing suggests that Hadid's architecture mediates Tatlin's sense of materiality along with the post-war aesthetics implied in Le Corbusier's *béton brut*. It could be that during the 1950s, there was an unconscious awareness of pitfalls in transforming the material into materiality when the project of modernity had already lost its historical drive, and image dominated the world of consumer culture. According to Roberto Gargiani, in the Swiss-French architect's shift for *beton brut, a psychological component also* urged Le Corbusier to see "in the roughness of the surface of his concrete, even the reflection of the aging skin of his own body."[74] In this light, Reyner Banham's juxtaposition of ethics with aesthetics of Brutalism was to introduce a rear-guard position in anticipation of the spectacle that would permeate the age of digital reproducibility when the line separating the cultural realm from the spectacular world of commodities is blurred.[75] As for contemporary architecture, the forgetfulness of the ethics in favor of aesthetics suggests that the spectacle Guy Debord attributed to commodities is tailored, reproduced, and personalized *ad infinitum* across the culture. And, "just when power—quite rightly because the spectacle shields it from having to take responsibility for its delirious decision—believes that it no longer needs to think; and indeed, can no longer think."[76] This historical framework has been taken up in this chapter to demonstrate "the kind of critical thinking that image can make possible."[77] The same theoretical paradigm demands historicizing Hadid's take on materiality as the image overtakes materiality.

In addition to the notion of *cut*, I would like to introduce what might be called the *economy of material*. Much has been said concerning the excessive use of steel in Herzog & de Meuron's "Bird's Nest," Beijing, 2008.[78] The building exemplifies many other works conceived and carried out in conjunction with digital technologies turning the structure into an ornament against the container quality of the building in analogy to a nest or a woven basket. A distinctive characteristic of similar projects is that their design disregards the local labor and techniques to attain "immateriality," as claimed by the architect, in a work that, by definition, is tectonic. Architecture as a commodity, like Marx's hypothetical wooden table, upon entering the market circle, "it changes into a thing which transcends sensuousness. It not only stands with its feet on the ground but, with all other commodities, it stands on its head and evolves out of its wooden brain grotesque ideas, far more wonderful than if it were to begin dancing of its own free will."[79] This might be one of the consequences of the globalization of architecture when star architects perform as master builders.

Star architects today conceive "design" as a system of information and transmission of external orders imposed on workers at the construction site.[80] This criticism should be reconsidered in light of a dialogue between Paul Valery and Auguste Perret. Asked why *not* build curved walls in concrete, a paste material, Perret drew the poet's attention to the influence of wood on classical architecture, when the material economy was considered an essential part of classical construction wisdom. Curved wooden forms have no precedent in classical architecture, but their contemporary use (from Perret's stand) is also costly. Despite Perret's paradoxical recoding of the trabeated structural system in concrete,[81] his rationale should be historicized. Firstly, in the everlasting structural image of wooden posts and lintel, its metamorphosis into monumentality, where the nature of the material (stone) is subdued at the expense of the Ur-form (archetype) of the original wooden hut. Secondly, because of—or despite—industrialization, most design strategies of early modernism had economic incentives—though delivered in the name of "form follows function," an idea borrowed from organic forms of nature in the first place. These observations by no means suggest that the *economy* is not a significant factor in today's architecture.[82] The severity of the current geopolitical situation, disguised by the rubric of austerity measures, speaks for itself. The invisibility of economic rationale today is due to the fluidity of image and its consolidation by the present regime of global capitalism. This turn of events has emptied the architecture of any social and collective agency, turning attention away from production at the expense of reception and consumption.

The notion of excess discussed earlier is the sole locale of material signification in architecture. Materials can be embellished to connote many things, including the aesthetic of monumentality, lightness or heaviness, ornamentation, and regional if not national identity. Ruskin's enthusiasm for the Venetian stones posited regional identity as the political agency of the century's debate on style. It was also a critical reflection on abstraction implied in Alberti's consideration of the column as ornament proper. Like most Renaissance architects, Alberti followed the classical discourse on material embellishment, which focused on column, frieze, base, and entablature architectonics. One consequence of this inclination toward these elements (mostly built-in stone) was to promote sculptural aesthetics Palladio avoided to a certain extent. Another one was to undermine surface ornament, *sgraffito*, which according to Alina Payne, had strong roots in Renaissance architecture.[83] Payne associates *sgraffito* with the transformation of surface motives from textiles to architecture as it unfolded in Florence. The city's silk trade with Mediterranean countries charged its architecture with regional identity. In introducing *sgraffito,* I wanted to draw the reader's attention to two implications of surface ornamentation for contemporary architecture. Elsewhere I have discussed the "return of surface" as one symptom of the commodification of architecture.[84] The present turn to surface embellishment unfolds a perception of

Figure 2.3 Peter Scott Cohen, Tel Aviv Museum of Art, 2011 (general view).

Source: Image courtesy of Amit Geron.

lightness and materiality that occasionally is dragged into regional and national identity politics. It is this second tendency that I want to conclude this chapter with.

Consider Pearson Scott Cohen's project for the Tel Aviv Museum of Art (2011) with apparent geometric similarity to Hadid's Phaeno Center (Figures 2.3 and 2.4). Both projects mediate between tectonics and the aesthetic of playfulness. Using the strategy of cutting and folding, both buildings use concrete for their structure and cladding elements. However, whereas in Hadid's project, materiality and cuts remain at the service of an image, they attain a geopolitical dimension in Cohen's work. From a distance, the texture of concrete in the Tel Aviv Museum of Art seems to simulate marble, a material the extensive use of which in government-sponsored buildings has promoted a sense of "national identity." In the Tel Aviv Museum, the concrete panels look like metal and marble through what the architect calls the aesthetic of "transmateriality." In Israel, according to Cohen, "this transitory quality means something more. Could it possibly represent new international secularism, dissociated from the national identity politics?" He continues, "Ultimately, the material resolution of buildings is among the most hotly debated issues we face. This is because it involves not only resources, but also politicized and conflicted positions held by different constituencies."[85] At this point, the suggested geometric similarity with the Phaeno Center is faulted because of excess in the envelope of Cohen's work is, writes Daniel Sherer, "more or less clearly understood set of aesthetic expectations tacitly established by precedent and the conjunction of artistic languages, ideological imperatives, and technological forces."[86] What we are facing

Figure 2.4 Zaha Hadid, Phaeno Science Center, Wolfsburg, Germany, 2000–05
(general view).

Source: Photograph by the author.

here is the state of contemporary architecture in non-Euro-America,
where the surface effects are not dictated merely by digital technology. A similar case, though with different strategies, can be pursued
in Wang Shu's design for the Ningbo Museum (Figure 2.5). In this
building, the traditional architectonic elements are functional and
ornamental. Experimenting with various materials, Wang Shu turns
the detailing into an image with connotations deeply rooted in the
local aspirations for substance, color, texture, and modernist visual
and tactile sensibilities. In his architecture, the tectonic of theatricality takes command transforming the material into materiality. To
save the radical potentialities of history, Wang Shu turns materiality into a critical strategy to re-write history. The image permeating
Shu's work recalls the Benjaminian "wish-image," pumping a new life
into the brick and other materials collected from the ruins left by
the "progress" the Chinese government champions. In addition to the
surrealist dimension of the Ningbo Museum, the tactile quality of
the building's brick cladding directs the spectator's gaze to the depth
of history—a reminder of the labor, tools, techniques, and builders'
desires to hold on to structures that are now destroyed. His strategic
approach to materiality is significant today when the "tool undergoes

Figure 2.5 Wang Shu, Ningbo Museum (general view).

Source: Photograph Courtesy of Wang Shu Architects.

metamorphosis and becomes more mental," and commodities con-
quer the solitude wherein the body used to experience the object.[87]

Interestingly enough, the concern for labor and traces of the hand
on the surface of the material that Ruskin preached is also evident
in Le Corbusier's postwar architecture. Most of his Brutalist phase
complements Perret's aforementioned paradoxical rationale. Le
Corbusier's use of surface *gauches* in the Marseille project, for example, pursues architectonic elements (the entry canopy and the rooftop
volumes), the geometry of which deviates from the orthogonal system
of the building. For him, "the construction process of concrete makes
it possible to see the handiwork of the craftsmen who take part in making the formwork and mold, as theorized by Ruskin or Tessenow."[88]
Whereas labor is central to articulating any material, what is exceptional about concrete used in sculpted architecture is its absence
in natural and industrial forms.[89] Concrete has no physicality (matter) like stone or wood, either. Neither has a historical precedent in
architectural history. To go beyond the engineering use of concrete,
most post-war Italian architects, for example, designed structures
that were *historically* hybrid.[90] Jean-Louis Cohen observes that Martin
Heidegger's suggestion that architecture is the result of "bringing
forth" the inherent natural qualities of stone and metal hardly can

be applied to concrete.[91] In Le Corbusier, *surface gauches* attempts to turn a functional element, the canopy, for example, into a supplement despite the orthogonal construction system. More relevant is Le Corbusier's midway meeting between European modernism and its importation to Chandigarh. According to Martino Stierli, this was not merely "the result of an export of architectural knowledge from Paris to the Panjab, but a project fundamentally shaped and enabled by the specific historical socioeconomic conditions on-site."[92] This aspiration for labor and materiality is subdued in most buildings produced since the turn to postmodernity, where the idea of image permeating postwar consumer culture is internalized into architecture. In the present age of digital reproducibility, we can conclude that the overpowering stature of the *image* has become detrimental to the visibility of labor and *material*, to the point that architecture reveals the very "look" permeating the fetishism of commodities.

Notes

1 Most mentioned is Semper's engagement in the design of the Canadian division. See Claudio Leoni, "Staging Canada: Gottfried Semper's Contribution to the Great Exhibition of 1851," in Michael Gnehm and Sonja Hildebrand, ed. *Architectural History and Globalized Knowledge: Gottfried Semper in London* (Madrid: Mendrisio Academy Press, 2022), 39–56.
2 Gottfried Semper (Der Stil), "Prolegomena," in Harry Francis Mallgrave & Michael Robinson, trans. *Style in the Technical and Tectonic Arts; or, Practical Aesthetics* (Los Angeles: The Getty Research Institute Publications Program, 2004), 75.
3 Leon Battista Alberti, De re aedificatoria (1486), *On the Art of Building in Ten Books*, trans. By Joseph Rykwert, Neil Leach, Robert Tavernor (Cambridge: The MIT Press, 1988).
4 Gottfried Semper, *Style in the Technical and Tectonic Arts; or, Practical Aesthetics*, transl. by Harry Francis Mallgrave and Michael Robinson (Los Angeles: Getty Research Institute, 2004), 250.
5 Kenneth Frampton, *Modern Architecture; A Critical History* (London: Thames and Hudson, 2007), 369–375.
6 Walter Benjamin, "The Work of Art in the Age of Mechanical Reproduction," in *Illuminations* (New York: Schocken Books, 1969), 221–224.
7 Walter Benjamin, "The Work of Art in the Age of Mechanical Reproduction," 1969, 221–224.
8 Giulio Argan, *The Baroque Age* (New York: Rizzoli International Publications Inc., 1989), 118–122.
9 Kenneth Frampton, "Intention, Craft, and Rationality," in Peggy Deamer and P. Bernstein, ed. *Building (in) Future: Recasting Labor in Architecture* (New York: Princeton Architecture Press, 2011), 28–37. Also see Peggy Deamer, *Architecture and Labour* (London: Routledge, 2020).
10 Hanna Arendt, *The Human Condition* (Chicago: University of Chicago Press, 1974), 140.

11 Zaha Hadid is highlighted throughout this essay because her work is exemplar of the aesthetic transformation of post-war brutalism to theatricalization. See Gevork Hartoonian, "Zaha Hadid: *Proun* Without a Cause," in *Architecture and Spectacle: A Critique* (London: Routledge, 2012), 145–172.

12 Adrian Forty, *Concrete and Culture* (London: Reaktion Books, 2012), 128.

13 Needless to say that these lines benefit from Walter Benjamin's "Experience and Poverty," written in 1933. See *Walter Benjamin: Selected Work, Volume 2, 1927–1934* (Cambridge: Harvard University Press, 1999), 731–735.

14 Compare Ruskin's statement with Adolf Loos, who said that one should paint wood any color but the color of the wood!

15 A classical case is Nikolaus Pevsner, *Pioneers of Modern Movement: From William Morris to Walter Gropius* (1936).

16 John Ruskin, *The Stones of Venice* (London: George Allen, 1905), 33.

17 Margaret Olin, "Self-Representation: Resemblance and Convention in Two Nineteenth-Century Theories of Architecture and the Decorative Arts," originally published in a German magazine in 1986. Here from http://www.jstor.org/stable/1482362 accessed 22/10/2013. Olin's presentation is focused on Gottfried Semper and Alois Riegl's writings on surface ornamentation with an emphasis on the concept of structural symbolism.

18 Marshall Berman, *All That Is Solid Melts into Air* (New York: Penguin Books, 1988).

19 Lars Spuybroek, *The Sympathy of Things: Ruskin and the Ecology of Design* (Rotterdam: NAI Publishers, 2011), 174–75.

20 See Italio Calvino, "Lightness," in *Six Memos for the Next Millennium* (Cambridge: Harvard University Press, 1988), 3–30. Milan Kundera, "Lightness and Weight," in *The Unbearable Lightness of Being* (New York: Harper and Row Publishers, 1984), 1–36.

21 Hal Foster, *The Art-Architecture Complex* (London: Verso, 2011), especially the chapter entitled "The Global Styles," 71–132.

22 Annette Fierro, *The Glass State: The Technology of Spectacle: Paris 1981-1998* (Cambridge: The MIT Press, 2003), 115.

23 Antone Picon, *The Materiality of Architecture* (Minneapolis: University of Minnoseta, 2020), 67.

24 Hubert Damisch, "The Space Between a Structuralist Approach to the Dictionary," *Architectural Design Profile*, vol. 3–4 (1980): 84–89.

25 Antone Picon, *The Materiality of Architecture* (Minneapolis: University of Minnesota Press, 2020), 31.

26 Mario Carpo, *The Alphabet and the Algorithm* (Cambridge: The MIT Press, 2011).

27 On Frank Gehry's architecture, see Gevork Hartoonian, "Frank Gehry: Roofing, Wrapping, Wrapping the Roof," in *Architecture and Spectacle: A Critique* (London: Routledge, 2012), 173–202.

28 Arantes Pedro Fiori, *The Rent of Form: Architecture and Labor in the Digital Age* (Minneapolis: University of Minnesota Press, 2019), 81

29 Antone Picon, *The Materiality of Architecture*, 2020, 120–21.

30 Leon Battista Alberti, *On the Art of Building in Ten Books*, trans. Joseph Rykwert, J., N. Leach, and R. Tavernor (Cambridge: The MIT Press, 1988), 35.

31 Quoted in Roberto Gargiani and Anna Rosellini, *Le Corbusier, Beton Brut and Ineffable Space, 1940–1965* (Lausanne: EPFL Press, 2012), 267. Le Corbusier spoke of "dignity of proportion" according to the author.

32 Gargiani and Rosellini, *Le Corbusier*, 267.
33 Akos Moravanszky, *Metamorphism: Material Change in Architecture* (Basel: Birkhauser, 2017), 8.
34 John Ruskin, *The Stones of Venice*, 31.
35 John Ruskin, *The Seven Lamps of Architecture* (New York: Farrar, Straus and Giroux, 1981), 39.
36 Gargiani and Rosellini, *Le Corbusier*, 267.
37 John Ruskin, *The Seven Lamps of Architecture*, 100.
38 Lars Spuybroek, *The Sympathy of Things: Ruskin and the Ecology of Design* (Rotterdam: V2_Publishing, 2011), 34.
39 Gottfried Semper, *Der Stil*, 2004, 97.
40 Gottfried Semper, *Style* (Los Angeles: The Getty Research Institute, 2004), 170–71.
41 John Ruskin, *The Seven Lamps of Architecture*, 15.
42 Harry Francis Mallgrave, "Introduction" to Gottfried Semper, *Style* (Los Angeles: The Getty Research Institute Publications Program, 2004), 53.
43 Gottfried Semper, *Style*, 2004, 97.
44 Gottfried Semper, "The Purists, Schematists, and Futurists," *Style*, 2004, 80.
45 Harry Francis Mallgrave, 2004, 53.
46 Gottfried Semper, *Style*, 2004, 97.
47 I am benefiting from Akos Moravanszky, *Metamorphism*, 2017, 226–228.
48 Gottfried Semper, "Prolegomena," *Style*, 2004; 77.
49 Alina Payne, "Bauhaus Endgame," in Saletnik J.S., Schuldenfrei, R., ed. *Bauhaus Construct* (London: Routledge, 2010), 259.
50 Alina Payne, "The Agency of Objects: From Semper to the Bauhaus and Beyond," in Ines Weizman, ed. *Dust Data: Traces of the Bauhaus across 100 Years* (Leipzig: Spector Books, 2019), 40.
51 Gottfried Semper, *Style* (Los Angeles: The Getty Research Institute, 2004), 529.
52 Gottfried Semper, *Style*, 2004, 645.
53 Gottfried Semper, *Style*, 2004, 731.
54 Gottfried Semper, *Style*, 2004, 371.
55 Harry Francis Mallgrave, 2004, 39–40.
56 Gottfried Semper, *Style*, 2004, 731.
57 See Claudio Leoni, "Staging Canada: Gottfried Semper's Contribution to the Great Exhibition of 1851," in Michael Gnehm & Sonja Hildebrand, ed. *Architectural History and Globalized knowledge: Gottfried Semper in London* (Zurich: gta Verlag, 2022), 39–56.
58 Gottfried Semper, *Style*, 2004, 438–439.
59 Gottfried Semper, *Style*, 2004, 250.
60 Gottfried Semper, *Style*, 2004, 218.
61 Akos Moravanszky, *Metamorphism*, 2017, 191.
62 Gottfried Semper, *Style*, 2004, 253.
63 See Kenneth Frampton's chapter on Louis I. Kahn in *Studies on Tectonic Culture* (Cambridge: The MIT Press, 1995), 209–246.
64 On the difference between theatricality and theatricalization, see Gevork Hartoonian, *Architecture and Spectacle: A Critique* (London: Ashgate, 2012).
65 On this subject, see Robin Evans, *The Projective Cast* (Cambridge: The MIT Press, 1995).
66 I have discussed Zaha Hadid's work in Gevork Hartoonian, *Architecture and Spectacle: A Critique* (London: Routledge, 2012), 145–172.

67 Jean-Louis Cohen, *The Future of Architecture Since 1889* (New York: Phaidon, 2012), 57.
68 Gargiani and Rosellini, *Le Corbusier,* 56.
69 Hubert Damisch, *Noah's Ark: Essays on Architecture* (Cambridge: The MIT Press, 2016), 187.
70 I recall James Stirling's reading of the French architect's work as quoted in Mark Crinson, *James Stirling; Early Unpublished Writings on Architecture* (London: Routledge, 2010), 128.
71 From a promotional email sent to this author's attention, August 17, 2012.
72 Cohen and Martin, *Liquid Stone,* 12.
73 Slavoj Zizek, *The Parallax View* (Cambridge: The MIT Press, 2006), 17.
74 Roberto Gargiani and Rosellini, *Le Corbusier,* 80.
75 For this author's discussion of the genesis of New Brutalism, see Gevork Hartoonian, *Footprint* (April 2009): 77–96.
76 Guy Debord, "XIII", *Comments on the Society of Spectacle,* trans. M. Imrie (London: Verso Books, 1988), 38.
77 T.J. Clark, *The Sight of Death* (New Haven: Yale University Press, 2006), 185.
78 This idea came up in discussion with Kenneth Frampton, and Wang Shu, the Chinese famous architect.
79 Karl Marx, Karl Marx, *Capital: A Critique of Political Economy,* vol 1., trans. Ben Fowkes (New York: Vintage, 1977), 163f.
80 Arantes Pedro Fiori, *The Rent of Form: Architecture and Labor in the Digital Age* (Minneapolis: University of Minnesota Press, 2019), 83.
81 I am paraphrasing Karla Britton, "Postscript: Perret's Critical Stance," in *Auguste Perret* (New York: Phaidon, 2001), 212–219.
82 See Arantes Pedro Fiori, *The Forms of Rent: Architecture and Labor in the Digital Age* (Minneapolis: The University of Minnesota Press, 2019).
83 Alina Payne, "Renaissance *sgraffito* Facades and the Circulation of Objects in the Mediterranean," in Annette Hoffmann, Manuel DeGiorgi, and Nicola Suthor, ed. *Synergies in Visual Culture* (München: Wilhelm Fink Verlag, 2013), 229–242.
84 See Gevork Hartoonian, *Architecture and Spectacle,* last chapter.
85 Ingeborg M. Rocker, "Distortion: An Interview with Pearson Scott Cohen," *Log,* vol. 24 (Winter-Spring 2012): 125.
86 Daniel Sherer, "The Historicity of the Modern," *Log,* vol. 24, 133.
87 Antonio Negri, *Art and Multitude* (Cambridge: Polity Press, 2011), 80.
88 Quoted in Gargiani and Rosellini, *Le Corbusier,* 43.
89 Adrian Forty, *Concrete and Culture* (London: Reaktion Books, 2012), 43–78.
90 Ibid., 98.
91 Cohen and Martin, *Liquid Stone,* 37.
92 Martino Stierli, "The Production of Concrete: Material Culture, Global Modernism, and the Project of Decolonization in India," in V. Prakash, M Casciato, and D.E. Coslett, ed. *Rethinking Global Modernism: Architectural Historiography and the Postcolonial* (London: Routledge, 2022), 279.

3 On Cladding

Starting with the Semperian motto that architecture is construction plus something else, this chapter explores the idea of excess encapsulated in Gottfried Semper's theory of *Bekleidung*, clothing.[1] Aside from an anthropological interest, Semper had an eye on the impact of the industrialization of buildings and the expressive dimension of materials such as iron and glass. To better understand his theory, it's essential to distinguish between the notion of cladding and covering each with aesthetic connotations, ranging from post-Renaissance and steel and glass architecture to the visibility of fashion in late nineteenth-century Europe. To demonstrate the relevance of the clothing concept for contemporary architecture, in addition to the historical coincidence between technological transformation unfolding today and during the late nineteenth century, we should also give attention to the phenomenal change of material to materiality, essential to architecture's uneven dialogue with time. At a general level, the alleged phenomenal concerns the transformation of stone, a natural matter, into an architectonic element with diverse tactile qualities accumulated throughout architectural history. In modern times, however, it involves re-coding the cultural sentiments associated with the aesthetic appropriation of the traditional perception of civic architecture in consideration to the spectacle paramount today. Apropos, the usefulness to re-think the Semperian notion of clothing in conjunction with the topicality of surface for the digitally reproduced architecture along with Le Corbusier's remarks on the surface and Adolf Loos's theorization of the principle of dressing. This retrospective reading will set the historico-theoretical premises to discuss the idea of cladding in contemporary architecture, working toward a critique of the digital reproduction of the surface as an image.

Semper and Loos's theorization of dressing should be differentiated from the "whitewash,"[2] parching the surface, a convention

DOI: 10.4324/9781003360445-4

practiced in vernacular and Mediterranean dwelling, and the classical notion of embellishment. If the former was part of an eco-ritual of annual cleansing of everything anew, a "productive morality,"[3] the classical case was primarily focused on the *surface* to produce appropriate compositional aesthetics rooted in the masonry building culture. Semper and Loos, each on a different temporal track, were concerned mainly with the element of the spatial enclosure, the one side of the wall contingent on the body in distinction to its representational side addressing the public. Whereas Loos's focus remained on the appropriateness of the cladding material to raise a particular sentiment relevant to the purpose of the enclosed space, Semper's dressing was tied to tectonics. This chapter aims to elaborate on various approaches to the surface, mapping the architectonic connotations of dressing, dressed-up, and covering.

At another level of consideration, if not for a better understanding of the various connotation of the *Bekleidung*, we should look at the facade-plan conversion in classical architecture. Since Roman times and through the architecture of seventeenth century Europe, when the column was conceived independent of the wall, the language of the Vitruvian Orders and their related motifs were stretched all over the main entry facade of civic buildings. Viewed frontally, the classical architecture looked as if it was conceived as a coherent language in a face-to-face dialogue with the public, bringing forth architecture's representational task while disguising its constructive dependency on the building's planimetric organization. As we noted in Chapter 1, the various designs proposed for the main façade of the Basilica San Lorenzo, Florence (1459) suggest that it was a common practice to conceive facades independently and after the completion of the building's construction, the masonry enclosure.[4] Even though Michelangelo's design for the San Lorenzo stood out without ever being built, in what follows, I would like to concentrate on his design for the Medici Chapel, and the Laurentian Library (1530) discussed extensively elsewhere.[5] The idea is to lay down the score clearly on the tectonics of the column and wall and the phenomenon of "thickening the wall" in Le Corbusier and Louis I. Kahn's architecture. The discussion also helps understand why Semper was skeptical of iron and steel's civic potentialities.

In the Medici Chapel (Figure 3.1), the representational association between architecture and sculpture supports, in the first place, the positionality of the sarcophagi and the statue of the deceased figure vis-à-vis the wall. In the second place, it highlights the role relief

Figure 3.1 Michelangelo, Lorenzo de' Medici Library, 1534 (interior view).
Source: Photograph courtesy of Hal Guida.

played in the "optical effect" of the overall composition. Notable in this configuration but also relevant to the tectonics of the column and wall is the figure of the recessed deceased in a niche, in analogy to the recessed columns of the vestibule of the Laurentian Library (Figure 3.2). The analogy departs from the column and body association, alluding to the myth of enlivening architecture at the expense of human sacrifice. Francesco di Giorgio shows "an immured maiden animating the architectural member," writes Alina Payne. According to her, the figures on relief, in addition to representing a narrative, also offer a "means of contributing to a phenomenology of the architecture. No matter how specific the story represented, the overall visual effect is that of organic animation of the wall surface."[6] The

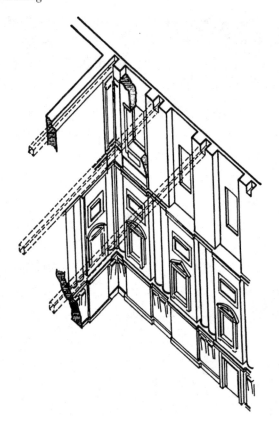

Figure 3.2 Structural system of the library vestibule.

Source: Reproduced from James Ackerman, *The Architecture of Michelangelo*, 1986. Copyright courtesy of Chicago University Press.

mythic root of organic animation in architecture also concerns the natural origin of masonry materials and the building's dependency on the landscape, no matter how techniques are abused to dematerialize architecture.

The notion of organic animation attains tectonic dimension in Renzo Piano's several works, in particular, Beyeler Foundation Museum-Riehen (Figure 3.3), discussed elsewhere.[7] Mention should also be made of Sean Godsell, an Australian architect who critiques the idea of "breaking the box" and makes ingenious attempts to animate the surface cladding. The movable panels of the roof in the House in the Hills open the interior space to the sky and horizon with an

Figure 3.3 Renzo Piano Workshop, Beyeler Foundation Museum-Riehen, Basel, 1991–2000 (roof image).

Source: Photo by Michel Denance.

eye on the suggested fourfold theatrical tectonics (Figure 3.4). In any event, back to Payne who considers these issues central to Alois Riegl's shift of interest from the courtyard to the palace's façade "as the Renaissance gradually morphs into the Baroque." Her observation also sheds a different light on Riegl's reading of these two works of Michelangelo, above all the centrality of themes such as surface, line, and the dialogue between column and wall, if not the column versus pilaster, and the treatment of the wall.[8] Interestingly enough, and as far as it concerns Baroque, Walter Benjamin wrote that the "conflict between sensibility and will result in the human norm," evident in Riegl's demonstration of the "discord between the attitude of head

Figure 3.4 Sean Godsell, The House in The Hills, 2020.

Source: Photograph by Earl Carter Photography, courtesy of Sean Godsell Architects, Melbourne, Australia.

and body in the figure of Giuliano and Night on the Medici tombs."[9] In Riegl's interpretation of Michelangelo's design intention, the paired columns of the vestibule of the Laurentian Library are presented as a relief—both in the literal sense of the word and Giuliano's figure a relief. We should, however, return to Payne and the element of relief in both the architect's and sculptor's drawings, where the planimetric section and the façade say two different things. While the relief in the plan is part of the expansion of the masonry construction system, later to be coined as "thickening the wall," the façade represents the classical rapport between the column and pilaster, with the wall the central support element of the edifice.

Thus, in both designs, Michelangelo repressed the tactile dimension of the wall's surface at the expense of creating optical depth and relief. I will further suggest that the Medici tomb's columns express *relief* from the anxiety caused by the Hellenistic juxtaposition of column and wall. Still, if one agrees with Riegl that Michelangelo is the founding architect of Baroque's representational system,[10] then the tentative separation of the column from the wall was Baroque's main contribution to the emancipation of the column from the wall—a shift which has the effect of "lightening the wall's load and mass," as suggested in Harry F. Mallgrave's reflection on Perrault's invented colonnade in the Louvre. I will return to Riegl's association between lines inscribed on the surface of the clothing of the sarcophagi and the intensification of the expressed emotions. But for the moment, we should stay focused on the figure of Giuliano, which is framed by double pilasters, a substitute for the recessed columns of the vestibule of Laurentian Library and endorsing the classical analogy between the column and the body promoted by Joseph Rykwert.[11] This much is also clear from James Ackerman's reading of the vestibule of Laurentian Library. According to Ackerman, Michelangelo altered the classical role of columns, which seem independent of architecture, like statues in the niches. At the same time, the projecting wall looks like supporting the ceiling. He wrote that, contrary to the canonical use of column as an ornament, Michelangelo's "invention is as essential to the stability of the structure as a Gothic pier."[12] The opposition between the structural function of column and wall and their visual effect lies in Riegl twisting the Semperian tectonics. To this end, we must now turn to Leon Battista Alberti's discourse on the column and wall.

In *De re aedificatoria* (penned 1452), Alberti suggests that the "whole matter of building is composed of lineaments and structure." And that the purpose of lineament is to define and articulate the surfaces of the building.[13] Alberti's remarks anticipated the importance of the wall and surface in Semper and Riegl's discourses. Equally noteworthy is Alberti's association of the column with ornament. In the Palazzo Rucellai, the distinction between the column and the wall has the least to do with their tectonic effect. Unlike the wall, the column has no role in covering space; in its singular standing, it underlines its loadbearing function. These two architectonic elements are presented as by-products of lineaments, and surface embellishment, issues Riegl would have considered an early attempt toward "autonomous representations of depth."[14] Alberti's association of the column with ornament is, however, paradoxical. Following Hubert Damisch's differentiation between "compliment" and "supplement," we should say that the Albertian column is a compliment in correspondence "to a possibility, even a necessity, inscribed in the object itself, which would remain incomplete without it." And that the relief as a supplement "remains external to the object to which it is added, just as sign remains external to the thing to which it is added."[15] The lineaments of the surface-face of the Rucellai building are not tectonic; it, however, perceptually anticipates the modern structural grid system. We should also say that, similar to the pleas of the clothing of the sarcophagi, the surface lineaments were expressive elements in dialogue with the absent spectator. It says more about the architect's exploration of how to further distance the wall architecture from the buttressed Gothic buildings. The architect's rapport with many facets of the object under design is one thing but to think of the object from the eye of the spectator is another. In contemporary architecture, particularly since the turn to the digital, the communicative dimension informing the triangulated relationship between the public, the object, and the architect is reduced to an image seen primarily from the eye of the spectator.

There is no column in Rucellai's main façade, but pilaster-looking surfaces are carved out of the building's surface cladding. This is not the case with the exterior elevations of Saint Peter's, for example, where what seems to be an undulating wall in the plan is transformed into the row of pilasters attached to the wall, the overall repetition of which evokes vertical expression. This tectonic reversal reaches its highest point in the building's dome, designed by Michelangelo circa 1534. In Riegl's words, "Buttresses, decorated at the front with paired columns, have been placed in front of the drum: these columns are not meant to please the eye, but rather symbolize through their coupling the effort necessary to carry the dome."[16] Still, each of the exposed buttresses of the dome stands on a pair of columns, the overall composition of which alludes to Gothic architecture if the masonry infill between them is removed.

Now, what brings together the architect, painter, and sculptor's drawings is the relief, a projected object to transcend the flatness of the drawing page (surface) with the difference that, in Michelangelo's drawings, the "quality of materiality and physical presence" discloses a carver's skills and sensibilities.[17] Central to Michelangelo's cut-out architectural profile is the flipping up of a plan drawing into a two-dimensional section or façade. It discloses the limitations of the delineation technique; however, it "needed to be translated into objects to be turned into three-dimensional forms on the stonecutter's table," writes Payne.[18] Further, she makes an interesting association between the transformation of two-dimensional profile drawings into three-dimensional objects with the artisanal techniques of tailors. Like architects and sculptors, tailors also spread the paper on the top of a fabric laying out the body's contours with chalk to mark the cuts and the pleats to be folded, a clothing relief. Whereas architectural and sculptural drawings must be handed to the builder or the stone cutter, the tailor performs both tasks. The tailoring techniques developed according to the body's posture attest to the actualization of the tailor's cut in the garment, in its double connotation as both technique and style (fashion). The artistry involved in covering and exposing the topology of the body with a fabric is the core idea in Semper's theory of clothing addressed in these pages.

To fully understand Semper's clothing theory, we should momentarily reiterate the aesthetics of the sculptor-architect's body-making skills and the corporeal nature of architecture. To this end, we should visit Kahn's First Unitarian Church of Rochester (1962–69). Aside from the tectonics of the sanctum expressed in its suspended-looking ceiling,[19] the vertical surface articulations of the building's façade are conceived in analogy to Gothic cathedrals using the technique of thickening the wall notable in the church's plan drawings and elevations (Figure 3.5). There are more layers involved in Kahn's take on the thickening of the wall than in Le Corbusier's Unite d'habitation, Marseille (1947–53), the progenitor of the idea, where the architect invests in the interactive rapport between the free façade, the piloti, and the slab. In contrast, Kahn remained focused on the wall's covering principle and the tectonics of the ceiling rather than the slab, if only to remain in accord with Semper's theorization of tectonics. If there are elements of classical architecture in the American architect's work, it is the absence

Figure 3.5 Louis I. Kahn, The First Unitarian Church, Rochester, NY, USA (exterior elevation).

Source: Image courtesy of the author.

of free-standing columns and thickened walls in the plan, perhaps in recollection of the walls of the Laurentian vestibule and pleas in costumes for aesthetic purposes, highlighting aspects of the body. If the thickening of the wall is essential for cladding, should we conclude that the digital turn to animated surfaces is a step toward the crisis of tectonics? Or should Semper's theorization of architecture be taken to critique the contemporaneity of architecture? The following pages are an historico-theoretical attempt to pursue the second option with an eye on the myth of Daphne pursued by Apollo. Spyros Papapetros demonstrates the usefulness of the tale of Daphne's metamorphosis into a figure of a tree a strategy to overcome humanity's limits and the "tendency to empathize with things that look like them," that is, the animated quality of the body for most.[20] As noted in the introduction to this volume, critical practice should pursue strategies to reverse the fetishistic animation of the surface and the evaporation of the physical body of architecture. The classical aesthetic analogy between building and the body is thus transgressed into a living organ, the surface of which not only curves around up and down but, thanks to computer programming, could also react to sound and light!

The Fabric of Dressing!

Two commonalities are recognized in most digitally reproduced architectural images: in appearance, they seem to challenge the traditional association between architectural form with nature, and Platonic geometries. The tendency to liquidate architectural form should be differentiated from early modern expressionism. Central to the formless expressionism of parametric is the return of the organic, discussed elsewhere.[21] The second feature of the digital architecture is to present a topographic perception of the surface, the primary task of which is to cover the space. While skin and its surface might be considered of particular interest to most organic forms, a different understanding of surface in architecture emerges if discussed in association with Semper's theory of *Bekleidung*, clothing. The German architect's genealogical link between tectonics and motifs originally generated in textiles is relevant to the critique of digital architecture advanced in this chapter. Having said this, there are commonalities between Semper's theorization of textiles and digitally operated architects. Of interest is Semper's explanation of the informativeness of stitches for producing embroidery, using the flat and the cross-stitches, and the criticality of *line* and *point* for flat stitch. And that plaiting and latticework were the ur-forms of the surface.[22] Aren't point, line, and surface stitched into the digital mechanism to keep with Semperian reading of the technical and aesthetic aspects of cultural artifacts, including architecture?

Exploring Semper's theory of clothing, I wish to highlight the tectonic rapport Semper grounds between the two elements of roof and enclosure, each with different surface articulations. Not only that these two elements should be considered as part of the surfaces enclosing a building, but it is also their demarcating line that contemporary architecture negotiates to produce flexible and, at times, animated undulating surfaces. Semper is also relevant because his idea of theatricality suggests critiquing the exhibitionistic tendencies of computer-generated forms and the aesthetic of commodity fetishism. The final section of this chapter will examine the contemporaneity of architecture wherein the surface emerges as a tectonic surrogate. Central to this observation is the conflation between the received aesthetics of both modern and pre-modern building culture and the image-making tendency promoted by the available media techniques. Similar to the last century, architecture today witnesses a more intensive technological influence on the perception of the work, its construction, reception, and fast-track transformation comparable to fashion. To further illuminate the conceptual difference between "dressing" and "dressed-up," essential for understanding Semper's theory of clothing, I will draw the reader's attention to examples from modern painting. Considering contemporary architecture's turn to topological surfaces, I will highlight the role organism plays in Semper's formulation of the tectonic. And that in analogy to the body, the organic is inseparable from the mechanic. Thus, the biological motifs permeating parametric are inundated by the mechanics of digital operation, networks that multiply the formal options of the grid. This last point sets the tone for a critical reading of contemporary architecture discussed in the chapter's final section.

Dressing the Body

I

A cursory review of the modern movement architecture suggests that, among other architects, Loos and Le Corbusier stand high in re-coding the received traditions of surface embellishment. Whereas Le Corbusier sympathized with the Loosian critique of ornament, how effective might a juxtaposition be between Semper and Le Corbusier, considering the commonality in Loos-Semper interest in dressing?

Even though there is not enough evidence whether Le Corbusier had read Semper firsthand,[23] he seems most likely would have agreed with Semper's interest in the dialectics between art and technique implicit in his theorization of style. Semper was familiar with the early nineteenth-century theorist Carl Friedrich von Rumohr, who popularized the term style, "pointing to the etymological link between the term style and the Latin term stylus, or writing instrument, the technical instrument with which the artist worked."[24] According to Semper, "In addition to the tool and the hand that guides it, there is the material to be treated, the formless mass to be transposed into form. In the first place, every work of art should reflect in its appearance, as it were, the material as physical matter." He then says, "Yet under the material, we understand something still higher, namely the task or the theme for artistic exploitation."[25] Is not the same message repeatedly underlined in Le Corbusier's *Vers une Architecture*, 1924, despite his expressed disappointment with Semper's Kunsthistorisches Museum during his 1911 visit to Vienna?

Before examining the Loosian idea of dressing, we should proceed with Le Corbusier's take on the surface subject. As early as 1911, in his travel diaries to Orient, then Charles-Edouard Jeanneret wrote that at Turnovo, "the rooms are whitewashed, and the white is so beautiful that I was very impressed. Already last year, I had become enthused over the decorative power that people and things take on when seen against the white of peasant rooms."[26] On two other occasions, Le Corbusier, touches upon the importance of the white surface that dominated his early work and vividly demonstrated this in his entry pavilion design for the occasion of the 1925 Decorative Arts exhibition, Paris. The pavilion is exemplar not only for its abstract white geometric look but its interior space as well. Seen from either side, the idea was to show "a certain look of cleanliness." Or "a cleaning the look, a hygiene of vision itself," writes Mark Wigley.[27] Making a representational correspondence between a Fernand Leger painting on the wall with a Thonet chair, the pavilion's split-level interior inaugurated a machine-time domestic space. A year before the event, Le Corbusier had published the French edition of *Vers Une Architecture*, one chapter of which was titled "Three Reminders to Architects," volume, surface, and plan.[28] Together, these can be taken for that "which is architectural in architecture," making the building distinct from painting and sculpture, the architect's two hubbies. Le Corbusier's account of the surface is brief; for him, the purpose of the surface is to cover the mass and respond to the energies of the internal volume and geometries of the mass. Juxtaposing the facade of the courtyard of San Damaso in the Vatican (captioned Bramante and Raphael) with examples of the factory and other engineering designs, Le Corbusier underlined the importance of maintaining a reasonable balance between openings, fenestrations, and the rest of the surface, which clothes the mass. Seemingly, only in this way is the mass left "intact in the splendor of its form in the light," along with the appropriateness of the surface for the utilitarian purpose of the volume and the opportunity to bring into the light the generating lines of the form. In all these and throughout the book, Le Corbusier had an eye on the work of engineering, projecting architecture that can stand up to it while appropriating both the technical and aesthetics of the machine age. However, I want to underline the implicit analogy between the mass's surface and the cloth covering the body. Similar to architecture, the dress covering the body unfolds an aesthetic dialogue between the exposed and protected parts of the body, a recurring theme in fashion.

II

Before turning to the second occasion, a detour is necessary to bring together the earlier discussion on the wall motif as part of the plan-sectional reversal in architecture evident in Le Corbusier's later work. In Notre-Dame du Haut, (1955), the curved facing wall in the plan bends outward, providing deep cuts for fenestrations. Whitewashed, the same thickened wall at one end slowly but expressively reaches out to the highest tip of its dark-colored roof as if holding it up (Figure 3.6). The design transforms the wall's horizontal extension into a vertical relief, projecting part of the wall out of its vertical plane and into the viewer's space. In addition to the technique of relief Michelangelo employed in his drawings,[29] this wall's theatricality recalls what Bernini employed in the colonnade in the Vatican studied by Le Corbusier. The wall "is not only curved, but it also faces toward the sky, so as not to constitute a vertical barrier and to encourage the penetration of light." Le Corbusier considered the wall's configuration "[the] third meaning of the folding surfaces when he justifies the choice of forms of Ronchamp as 'an answer to the psychophysiology of the feeling.'"[30] According to the authors, using the technique of gunite projected concrete, the architect could set up *surfaces gauches* different from those of engineering. Discussing how painting and sculpture support each other representationally, Semper wrote, "Next came all the architectural forms that we now call moldings (*moulures*), which includes everything that was not

Figure 3.6 Le Corbusier, Ronchamp, Notre-Dame de Haut, 1955, France (exterior view).

Source: Photograph courtesy of Shuyen Ee.

dictated by construction."[31] What happens in this particular case is not dissimilar to Greek art, which according to Riegl, "Pattern and ground separate, and the figures now characterized in as three-dimensional, emerge diagonally from the ground."[32] The same figurative motif is at work in the Unite d'habitation, Marseille (1952), where, as we noticed, the surface covering the front and rear sides of the building are thickened. It creates a three-dimensional motif stretched horizontally and vertically, in analogy to the split-level interior spaces of each apartment (vertical) and the corridor running in between (horizontal). We should extend this observation to include Kahn's Salk Institute, with the building's thickened surfaces creating relief projecting out of the surface of the exterior walls. In these briefly discussed works, both architects recode the traditions of flat surface embellishment, creating architectonic motifs in tandem with a different aesthetic-technique paradigm. Should we conclude that the infrastructural nature of the suggested horizontal and vertical axis is internal to architectural dressing and the transformation of a building into civic architecture?

In *The Decorative Art Today,* Le Corbusier juxtaposes technique and aesthetics to highlight the cleaning power and energy of the machine age. He writes, "On white ripolin walls, these accretions of dead things from the past would be intolerable: they would leave a mark. The marks do not show on the medley of our damasks and patterned wall-papers."[33] In the same pages, he expresses his love affair with the Mediterranean architecture he visited during his journey.[34] And he pens his sympathy with the modern times in the following words: "In the course of my travels, I found whitewash whenever the twentieth century had not yet arrived," and that wherever industry has conquered, "the traditional whitewash will be replaced by wall-papers, gilt porcelain, ..." and other products identified with industrially produced decorative arts. Nothing short of this says about his interpretation of the modern age and the architecture put on a show in the Weissenhofsiedlung at Stuttgart, a Werkbund exhibition of 1927, a collection of residential buildings designed by architects soon to be identified with the international style architecture. At the time of this exhibition, the displayed white architecture stood out against the presumed "dark" context of the prevailing tendencies, decorating objects disregard to their utilitarian purpose.

Interestingly enough, in a caption for a photo of Sultan Mahembe and his two sons, Le Corbusier wrote, "Three black heads against a white background, fit to govern, to dominate ... an open door through which we can see true grandeur."[35] He will take up the suggested visual contrast in a promotional strategy for his Villa Stein; the picture's forefront is occupied by a black automobile and a female fashionably dressed in white. It is useful to reflect on the reversal between white and black color in these two images: Wigley writes, "The impact of modern architecture depends a lot on whether its white surfaces appear against a background of color or the color appears against a background of white."[36] Further interest is the precision evident in the displayed car, the Villa, and the female's dress cut. In retrospect, it is not far-fetching to say that the Villa and the dress in the picture look more modish and advanced than the car. Arantes Pedro Fiori summarizes the paradox in this way: "the production of an immovable manufactured commodity proved to be unexpectedly flexible (mobile), while the production of a mobile commodity in the Fordist industrial era became standardized and invariable (immobile)."[37] This difference is floated today thanks to digital infusion into every design production activity. Smooth undulating shapes cover up-scaled cars and corporate architecture alike.

Loos established a different rapport between fashion and surface. In "The Principle of Cladding," he gives a new twist to Semper's idea of dressing. For Loos, the first task of the architect is to embellish the dressing material with tactile qualities that would evoke a particular sentiment. The second task of the architect, he wrote, is to think of a structure to hold the enclosure, the four carpets implied in Semper's theory of dressing. There is a rift between Semper and Loos's interpretations of dressing even though both underline the primary task of dressing to cover the space. Both architects' discussion of dressing implicitly recognizes the masonry wall's dual surface, its two faces. While Semper wanted to underline the covering principle of textile, essential to Loos is the materiality of the inner face of dressing that should be coordinated with other interior surfaces and even with the type of chairs and tables together creating a familiar atmosphere, recollecting bygone tactile sentiments of materiality accumulated in the culture of building. On the other hand, regarding the dressing material and its outer face, Loos differed from Le Corbusier even though the latter was sympathetic to Loos' seminal text, "Ornament and Crime,"[38] written in 1908 and published in Le Corbusier's *L'Esprit Nouveau* in 1920. We have already noticed Le Corbusier's puritanic aesthetics and should be recalled along with what Loos had to say about fashion and garments. According to him, the German asks whether a man is dressed "beautifully," whereas the Englishman laughing at the German's esteem with beauty, asks whether he is dressed "well" or "correctly."[39] Critically challenging the Viennese Secessionist work, he continued, the gentleman seeks not to be shining out but remain inconspicuous, attired adequately for a given function, from bicycling to a formal occasion. Herein, the Semperian notion of dressing, the lawful surface embellishment central to the distinction he made between tectonics of theatricality and theatricalization. The same goes with Loos's assertion that we should paint the wood any color except the color of the wood. Loos' principle of dressing was to highlight the distinction between the tactile quality of the interior dressing from the exterior, which most often (to add another difference with Le Corbusier) benefited from the pre-modern masonry culture of building. Their differences are essential: most of the interior spaces of Loos's houses are cladded with materials and objects alluding to a particular aura distinct from the visual world of the metropolis. Le Corbusier instead was to internalize the abstract experience of the metropolis into the domestic domain. There goes the differences between the open-plan and the raum-plan as well.[40]

That fashion and dress are central to modernism are apparent today when the fleeting nature of commodities, to recall, Charles Baudelaire is part of the everyday life experience permeating most metropolitan cities.[41] What makes the subject of further interest is that even in its most fleeting moments, the dress is cut and fashioned about the topology of the body. The body is indeed the *ur-form* of clothing, as is the core-form for the art-form. Three examples of dressing are presented here to cement the tectonics involved in covering the body and to underline the obvious; after Semper, as will be demonstrated shortly, we should claim that, while all products of textile are based on a Cartesian grid structure, the very art-form of fabric, including its color, texture, and figures are woven into the fabric of that structure. In textiles and ceramics, according to Semper, we "find the first efforts to embellish functional objects through conscious choice of form and decoration."[42] He continues that the cut and pleats sought for the covering should highlight the properties of that which is covered. Therefore, the surface is not an abstract veneer both in fabric and in the surface covering of architectural space. Still, a tectonic figuration is conceived according to the purpose and convenience of the building's purpose. In addition to an interest in anthropology, Semper's clothing theory was primarily concerned with how the core-form (the constructed mass) is artistically expressed in the art-form, the lawful articulations of the surface. While the general topology of the body remains constant, what makes the following three types of clothing different is the purpose each is cut for and how this consideration prompts a further tectonic articulation of the cut and style, that is, fashion. Semper demonstrates how the ornaments on the Egyptian capital were borrowed from motifs developed in costume and finery.[43] With this difference in mind, we can see that the digitally produced animated surfaces have no relevance to the Semperian or Loosian formulation of dressing; they are objectile that have internalized the fetishistic nature of commodities.

The two extremes of the three clothing examples should be mentioned first. A swimmer or diver's wetsuit is cut and designed strictly in terms of the speed and mobility of the body in the swim. Carnival dress, in contrast, is primarily designed to look spectacular. The surface in the former is attached to the body's skin, exaggerating those parts of the body that are covered. The carnival dress relates to the body through axillary armatures, the structure of which is sought in the dress's final form and surface appearance. In both examples, purpose and use remain essential though perceived towards two different ends. In the wetsuit, the body's structure informs the form and its surface. In the carnival dress, the body disappears behind clothing. One might say that in the wetsuit, the body is dressed, while in the second example, the body is dressed up.[44] The third dressing example is the excellent and regular clothes worn by men and women, the design of which is not blind to fashion and its stylistic variations. Consider the woman's dress in the earlier mentioned photo of Le Corbusier's Villa Stein and a rendering of Otto Wagner's second Villa, Bujattigasse, Vienna, designed in 1905. This Villa's cubic purity is further highlighted against the materiality of the sitting and the passing couple dressed elegantly and modern.

Contrary to Wagner's earlier work, the dressing of this villa was conceived with an eye on articulating the rising construction systems while accommodating selected artistry and surface embellishments from the culture of building.[45] What makes the third type of dressing of interest is that similar to tectonic forms, it is the cuts, pleats, and openings that fashion the surface of the fabric and dramatize it aesthetically by revealing and concealing the body, whose covering is the primary task of clothing, even when nudity is exploited for visual and sexual delight. More specifically, it is the line marking the knee, the torso, and the shoulder that, in most cases, is used and abused to facilitate fashion's move from one style to another. And yet, while fashion and surface are mainly interwoven, if not in *organic* rapport with each other, what remains central to the technique of covering are two that, according to Semper, constitute the basics of any act of making.

To further highlight the differences between dressed-up and dressing, it is helpful to recall two paintings, Rene Magritte's *Philosophy in the Boudoir* (1947) and Gustav Klimt's painting *The Kiss* (1908). Of interest are the clothing style and its contribution to the artistic purpose of both images. While in Magritte, the nudity is depicted in the translucent nature of the fabric covering the body's morphology, in *The Kiss*, the emphasis is put instead on the representational dimension of the painting at the expense of the body's disappearance behind the clothing. To make the difference clearer, we must introduce Alois Riegl's notion of *Stimmung* (mood or atmosphere) to reconcile "optical values" and the reality depicted in Klimt's painting called Die Philosophie, which was commissioned for the ceiling of the department of philosophy building and was destroyed in 1900.

The significance of Riegl's exploration of Stimmung, writes Margaret Olin, "is that it sought to incorporate an aspect of art Riegl regarded as suspicious and unsatisfying, optically, into scientific casualty, even if it did so with some reservations."[46] This discussion on the "appearance" can also be extended to compare two famous structures of the nineteenth century: the Eiffel Tower and the Statue of Liberty. In the latter, the representational intention is the main form-giving element of the surface. Like carnival clothing, the statue's physical body, its structure, is hidden behind the fabric. In utilizing the surface for image-making, the way fabric relates to the body is pushed into shadow. Most perforations in the surface of the Eiffel Tower, instead, function structurally and address that which, to Semper, constitutes the art-form of the tectonic. Accordingly, the relationship between the representational and structural in the Eiffel Tower is organic. This observation offers another way of differentiating the idea of dressing from the dressed-up.

Now, the surface remains essential for covering and protecting (vertical), whereas similar to the planimetric composition, what articulates the surface of any covering is of linear nature (horizontal). Against abstract formalism of the neo-avantgarde work of the 1980s and the simulated historical forms of postmodern architecture, the tectonic highlights the lines and pleats that structure the surface, not for the sake of beauty and fashion but to reveal the *structure* behind the cover artistically. To highlight the linear elements of any architectonic form, the architect should do more than restore the Cartesian grid implied in the element of walling (the vertical) and roofing (the horizontal). The wall should expressively articulate its support for the roofing. Thus, the tectonic significance of "binding" and the possibility of a surface architecture woven of linear elements much like a basket. For Semper, the most complex tectonic forms articulate the surface of covering with linear elements rather than employing illusive animated surface plates visible in most digitally reproduced works.

Building Surfaces

Any discussion concerning the tectonic rapport between wrapping and roofing involves examining the historicity of these two architectonic elements. Recent architectural theories discuss "surface" about the visual aesthetics of media technologies with a vague reference to Semper. As noted previously, in "Digital Semper,"[47] Cache dwells on Semper's theory of dressing without taking note of the difference between "surface" and the idea of dressing, as well as the difference between dressing and the dressed-up. The dressed-up suggests wrapping a constructed form with surfaces that might evoke a particular style or symbolism of the kind in vogue during the late 1970s eclecticism or current tendencies for theatricalization. In contrast, Semper's theory of dressing is primarily concerned with the artistic articulation of the material of the outer clothing (*Bekleidung*), evoking the load-bearing elements. For Semper, the "hanging carpets remained the true walls; they were the visible boundaries of a room. The solid walls behind them were necessary for reasons that had nothing to do with the creation of space; they were needed for protection, for supporting a load, for their permanence, etc."[48] Nevertheless, it is the patterns of the so-to-speak carpet that in due time was used as lineaments covering the masonry wall. Cache takes Semper's theory to justify the current turn to the surface as a thin film covering a geometric form (blob) or a digitally manufactured textile-like fabric hung from a frame structure or morphed into a topographical architecture (fold). Seemingly, the digital turn to Semper draws analogies between the materiality of textile and the way it was produced with digital manufacturing. Starting with the Semperian knot, Cache foregrounds the notion of objectile, "an open-ended notation which allows for infinite parametric variations."[49] The missing points are two; firstly, the tectonic theory designates multiple inner associations between the art-form, core-form, on the one hand, and the earth-form and the frame-work on the other, as mapped in the introduction. Secondly that any technically centered re-coding of architecture stops short of historicizing the current visual and tactile experiences along with the disciplinary history of architecture. To further clarify these observations, it is useful to review Semper's theory of dressing closely.

In the "Preliminary remarks on polychromic architecture," Semper argues that unpretentious lavishness is a natural need for architecture if the whole matter is treated artistically. According to him, this conditional endorsement of excess is fulfilled when, as in the ancient Greek monuments, the architect combines painting, sculpture, and other arts to create a chorus.[50] Juxtaposing dance and fine arts, Semper wrote "Art knows only one master: Necessity," and that one should handle such a subject artistically using available architectonic elements. The idea of necessity was critical for nineteenth-century architecture in more ways than one: a practical understanding of the socio-cultural consequences of the industrial revolution, the emergence of new building materials, and typologies were instrumental in generating esteem for Realism and "objectivity," which was shared by many architects and artists.[51] Following Carl Bötticher's distinction between the core-form and the art-form, Semper observed that the "beginning of building coincides with the beginning of textiles" and that, in early civilization, carpets used to enclose the interior space were hung from a frame that fulfilled the structural and practical needs.[52] According to him, the carpet's motifs were later conceived as a stylistic or tectonic surrogate, first applied in the building's floor design. Its motifs were then transformed into the building's dressing, as noted above. Two points should be highlighted here. Firstly, the scaffolds used to support the draperies to enclose and divide the space had nothing to do with the initial spatial concept of the building. Secondly, in the transformation (*Stoffwechsel*) of various surface motifs produced in applied arts, Semper distinguished between excess that had structural origin and motifs that, according to him, are "tendentious art which has nothing in common with the structure and technical assembly of the work." Here Semper discusses the frame-work as a means of supporting the roof and shows how the dressing might impinge on it as if competing with the tectonics of the frame-work. In his words, "the free will of the creative human spirit is the first and most important factor in the question of the origin of architectural styles, although, of course, man's creative power is confined by certain higher laws of tradition, demand, and necessity."[53] The implied historicity alludes to the emerging Realism that even Otto Wagner's "utility-style" (Nutz-stil) could not but comply with restrains denoted in Semper's sentence.

To further clarify the restrain involved in the artistic articulation of the core-form, it is useful to recall Semper's two genealogical assumptions: first, that textiles are the progenitor of the architectural motif. For him, the masonry wall evolved through a sequence of spatial enclosures; primitive screen or woven-matt, then metal sheathing, and eventually carpets whose colorful textures were applied to the surface of a masonry building to evoke a sentiment of civic architecture if not monumentality.[54] Second, Semper was concerned with the difficulty involved in the artistic use of iron for monumental architecture. His argument also responded to those who believed Greek architects shunned using color in monuments. Dwelling on necessity, Semper argued for a concept of dressing to wrap the structure, the core-form, in an art-form that might deny the material basis of the former. According to him,

> architecture could only attain a pivotal status among the fine arts by elevating the "poetic idea" of the building's purpose (using types, metaphors, and functional forms) to such a level that the

physical material of the building disappeared from the subjective consciousness, leaving only the contemplation of its transcendental meaning.[55]

This statement discloses Semper's re-interpretation of the nineteenth-century drive for realism and objectivity with an eye on the disciplinary history of architecture.

There were other interpretations of "necessity" as the nineteenth century ended. As noted earlier, Wagner discussed Realism in terms of faithfulness to modern life's material and practical demands. In defense of *Nutz-Stil*, he underlined the French experience where the architect functioned as an artist and building technician. Further, considering realism in French painting, he wrote, "such Realism in architecture can also bear quite peculiar fruit."[56] However, challenging Semper's theory of *Bekleidung*, Wagner came short of proposing a clear alternative to how architecture attains a particular art-form from a given structural system. His early views recall Marc-Antoine Laugier's interest in the rational expression of construction. As Peter Haiko reminds us, Wagner's later practice unfolds a tectonic form in which the actual structure often remains hidden. In the main façade of Postsparkasse, the nails adorning the façade were not used to visualize the structure per se, "but of that which reminds us of it … The task of the bolts is to point out to the viewer the novelty of the encasement, namely the slabs, to make it obvious and eternal."[57] Surface semantics invested in Wagner's tectonic were mainly motivated by the physical material of construction. In St. Leopold church, Wagner re-coded the traditional form of construction. Here bolts are used to "hold the cladding panels, even their lightness, but at the same time bears the marks of the building's duration."[58] Should the "realism" of the bolts be associated with iron structures and J. J. Winckelmann's belief that the stone construction system drove the poetics of Greek temples? Questioning the rationalist distinction between the structural and the ornamental, Semper's discourse on dressing, instead, levels architecture with dance and music. He coined architecture as a cosmic art. Music and dance differ from the imitative arts in that it is almost impossible to distinguish between what is essential to them and what is excessive or ornamental. The implied idea of theatricality and its correspondence to the Greek chorus and dance suggests that excess in architecture should be the architect's conscious attempt to plot architecture within a broader cultural experience. And yet, central to the idea of theatricality is the embellishment of the constructed form to the point of mastering the material, denial of its matter. Reflecting on the dramatization evident in ancient theatrical masks, Semper wrote that the form fakes if there is nothing behind the mask. And, "Every artistic creation, every artistic pleasure, presumes a certain carnival spirit, or to express it in a modern way, the haze of carnival candles is the true atmosphere of art. The destruction of reality, of the material, is necessary if form emerges as a meaningful symbol, an autonomous human creation."[59] Accordingly, theatricality is integral to the schism between the core-form and the art-form and the lawful articulation of the surface material. What has become a burden for most architects today is how to think of architecture in conjunction with a "broader cultural experience" after the loss of aura and at the time when animated images (theatricalization) are digitally reproduced and consumed globally.

Semper's idea of theatricality is essential in the light of the accusation that he was a die-hard materialist,[60] as part of several confusing views on Semper's discourse. Wagner made a case out of Semper's discourse on style, criticizing the architect's preference for symbolic over material factors. Following Riegl's idea of *Kunstwollen*, Peter Behrens, among others, chastised Semper for the alleged mechanistic views of the essence of art,[61] even though he could not but agree with Semper that style "is not shaped by individual taste, technique, or material," an idea Behrens promoted in his essay, "Art and Technique."[62] Still, in the debate between Riegl and Semper, most contemporary art historians take side with the former. Benjamin Binstock argues that in *Der Stil*, Semper "proposed that the style of an artwork was determined by function, material, and technique. Riegl acknowledged the importance of these factors but insisted on something prior and more crucial," finding "a middle ground between the unfolding of Spirit on the one hand and function or technique on the other in the formal elements of the work of art *as art*, ... "[63] In contrast, Semper attempted to draw one's attention to that aspect of architecture that, like other commodities, has to do with the realm of consumption. To be "attractive," like products of fashion, and to be appropriated by the masses, like every other modern product, architecture should constitute "antiquity anew out of the most recent past." According to Peter Osborne, "As objects of fetishization, commodities destined for everyday consumption display two closely related features: one is an apparent self-sufficiency or independence from their process of production; the other is the appearance of novelty, required to make them attractive in the face of competing products."[64] The implied dialogical relation between past and the present demonstrates Semper's inclination to bring architecture together with other cultural products, including motives produced by the applied arts such as weaving and ceramics, but also dance and chorus, material experiences that are absent in Wagner's discourse on realism. If it is dismissed that the tectonic involved in the artistic articulation of the dressing of a constructed form, then, similar to the examples of clothing explored before, the purpose of the art-form might be reduced just to deliver motifs that are fashionable across the cultural realm, *spectacle* as is the case today.

Besides Semper's belief that fabrication is essential to architecture's interiority, what Semper wrote and built were charged, in a disguised way, with a glimpse of what has become a century later an experience of everyday life;[65] that is, the permeation of the aesthetic of commodity fetishism. The totalization implied in Semper's idea of theatricality is relevant to contemporary architecture when dissimilar to Loos and Le Corbusier it is not orchestrated by re-coding received traditions but by animated surfaces in two primary forms, the fold and the blob architecture.[66] What the blob, a generic name for the computer-generated form, offers is not the new but a sense of aesthetic appreciation that runs through the entirety of the present spectacle culture. To further understand the difference between "dressing" and "dressed-up," the historicity of organic forms implied in the digital turn should be addressed next.

Surface Organic[67]

To historicize the digitally reproduced architecture, we should attend to two interrelated observations. On the one hand, any architectural criticism today should consider the "return of organic" and distinguish between "theatricalization" and Semper's tectonic of theatricality, a concept he used to critique the un-lawful excess in architecture. However, what he and Loos could not accept in the Viennese secessionist work has taken today a new turn is the sheer ideological coincidence between the aesthetic of commodity form and the exuberant digitally reproduced architecture. This turn of events has replaced the Semperian dressing with animated surfaces. Paradoxically, suppose the secessionist movement was reacting partly against the rising materialistic tendencies and the drive for objectivity. In that case, the theatricalization in today's architecture is engineered by the *machine,* the etymology of which, interestingly enough, aspires to organic.

Starting with the body, there is merit to recalling the Latin *organicus* that did not "mean anything very different from mechanicus:

something is done using instruments indirectly."[68] Accordingly, implied in the Corbusian house-machine analogy is the correct handling of organicism, the body's engagement with edifice's horizontal and vertical spaces. And yet, the return of organic today should also be understood in conjunction with the near history of organic in architecture. Criticizing the totalizing tendency of the international style architecture, Peter Collins presented "biological analogy" as one paradigm among four others, framing the horizon of his discourse advanced in *Changing Ideals in Modern Architecture* (1965). Caroline van Eck also discusses the significance of organicism for nineteenth-century architecture; it offered "a strategy of invention, by which stylistic decisions are made and justified, or as a strategy of interpretation, through which the meaning of architecture, and especially the architecture of the past, can be formulated."[69] In any event, we should revisit Collins' paradigm in the light of organic permutations in digital architecture that might be taken for the work of modern expressionists or Frank L. Wright's organic theory. In place of what has been said, I argue that neither of these two tendencies of modernism has the least commonality with the subjectivity vested in current biomorphic forms.

Since antiquity, to follow Semper,[70] in addition to plant and animal forms, human figures were utilized for symbolic and structural ends. While Semper's observation concerned the organic idea implied in the tectonic articulation of ornament and structure, his following remarks are relevant to the current obsession with surface architecture. For Semper, the organic content of the tectonic in Greek Orders was anticipated in the Assyrian column, though without the "animating spark of Prometheus" to present a perception of surface-shell. Following Semper and paraphrasing him, I argue that in many blob mutations, the function of the structure is infused into the shell, and the "structural scheme and the artistic scheme are one," and that "organic" haunts the image. There are numerous examples of contemporary architecture where the enveloping shell approximates the tectonics, similar to a woven mat (Zaha Hadid, Opera House, China) or a basket (Herzog & da Meuron, Beijing Olympic Stadium, the nest!).[71] Anthony Vidler correctly characterizes the architects' interest in the Deleuzian fold as part "of conscious literalization, deployed in the service of an architecture that takes its authority from the inherent 'vitalism'—of computer-generated series." The strategy entitles the architect "to see the Deleuzian model as an invitation for a rather literal folding of the envelope, a complex curving of the skin, that tends to ignore rather than privilege the interior."[72]

Looking like another blob, the organic in Son-O-House benefits from Lars Spuybroek's reading of John Ruskin's theorization of the Gothic. In comparing the architecture of Gothic with the classical, the Dutch architect argues that "The Gothic body is what these days we would call a fractal body, a body of splittings, extensions, and continuous breaks."[73] Inspired by the Gothic column splitting into woven ribs covering the ceiling, he considers the Gothic cathedral construction par-excellent rather than representational, as suggested in Bötticher's distinction between the art-form and the core-form. In the Deleuzian fold system, Spuybroek writes, "continuity always proceeds singularity, while in the rib system, entities precede continuity."[74] The missing point in various ideological returns to the organic is to domesticate the shock effects and anxieties unleashed by late capitalism. This techno-visual culture has moved beyond the modernist aesthetic of abstraction and the flux induced by the globalization of capital and the information industry, a network covering the globe. To naturalize the very mechanistic logic of computer technology, the digital turn covers an exact form with surfaces that simulate the bygone zoological and landscape forms implied in the word "tectonics." Even though there has been a tendency to "anthropomorphize the material world" or "humanize nature" in the ancient sculptures evident in the great collections of natural and human objects, Horst Bredekamp writes, "automatons were the most obvious expression of the desire to imitate life by inspiring movement."[75] Nevertheless, there is a difference between the morphing body of architecture and buildings, let alone ancient sculpture, which should not be dismissed. Consider this, within the torn-apart landscape of the pre-modern world, the white and abstract forms of the early modern buildings stood aloof and looked surreal, less popular. Today, thanks to the infusion of digital reproducibility in every design process, the comparison between the advanced look of early modern architecture and an automobile are flattened; the aesthetic of the spectacle covers all surfaces regardless of the purpose of the object. The earlier last century's organic theories of architecture and the work of expressionism were responding to the rising metropolis and a straitjacket understanding of functionalism. We should extend the historicization outlined here toward a critical assessment of contemporary architecture.

The presented historico-theoretical proposition provides a lens to look at the predicament of contemporary architecture, which is structured by roofing and wrapping, two ontological elements in Semper's theorization of dressing. Accordingly, the dialogue between the

horizontal and vertical not only should be re-thought in consideration of the tectonic rapport between the earth-work and the frame-
work, but also the role dressing plays when a strict demarcation of
roofing over clothing (R. Piano, Beyeler Foundation, Figure 3.3),
or vice versa (F. Gehry, Disney Concert Hall, Figure 3.7) is blurred.
These and other architects, including Peter Eisenman, are discussed
elsewhere.[76] However, it's worth mentioning that Eisenman's strategy
utilizes fabric to separate the interior space from the outside. And yet,
instead of articulating the tectonic rapport between the enclosure
and the structure, he seemingly agrees with Loos that the support
element is secondary to the idea of wrapping. Apropos, Eisenman's
move to recoding the concept of dressing. Similar to the work of a

Figure 3.7 Frank Gehry, Walt Disney Concert Hall, Los Angeles, CA, 1997–2003.

Source: Image courtesy of the author.

tailor, his design process involves laying down a virtual matt, proceeding towards the formation of an object that meets the horizon of the landscape and the verticality of the body midway. Eisenman's turn to landform is inspired by Georges Bataille's remarks on alteration, another term associated with Semper's interest in textiles.

In discussing the surrealist artwork, Bataille's idea of alteration meant a strategy to recode classical dualities like high and low and base and figure. Thus, the possibility to place the work between devolution and evolution.[77] In the process of transgression, the "surface" emerges as a symptom of horizontality, if not the "flatbed picture plane" discussed by Leo Steinberg. Accordingly, "the flatbed picture plane" transforms art's subject from nature to culture and avoids perceiving the world from an upright position. Discussing several American painters of the 1950s, Steinberg concludes that "the flatbed picture plane lends itself to any content that does not evoke a prior optical event. As criteria of classification, it cuts across the terms 'abstract' and 'representational.'"[78] In Eisenman's architecture, space is perceived in the interplay between surfaces needed to wrap the interior space and the play of tectonics. To put it differently, the physicality of Eisenman's architecture is fissured in the diagrammatic representation of the site's topography and the program.

Given the available materials, building techniques, and programmatic needs, Eisenman reiterates the ethos of avant-gardism and yet resists falling into the trap of the *Zeitgeist* entertained by architects who reduce architectural form to the images generated by electronic technologies. Operating in a tightrope zone, Eisenman wishes to recode the early modernist formalist ethos according to contemporary mental life. The Staten Island Institute of Art and Science (Figure 3.8) project addresses architecture's relation to a society deeply entangled with the spectacle of late capitalism. His work involves readjusting architecture's interiority to illuminate the difficulty of retaining critical distance from the theatricalization of architecture, and submitting the art of building to the aesthetic of commodity fetishism. In arguing that wrapping and roofing are formative for a critical engagement with the predicament of contemporary architecture, the aim is to say something more than putting one particular architect against others: we are witnessing a historical situation where Semper's discourse on theatricality might be taken to affirm the present culture of spectacle. Furthermore, if it is still helpful to claim that Mies van der Rohe exhausted the tectonic potentialities of steel and glass architecture,[79] is it not necessary to explore the dialogical

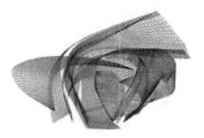

Figure 3.8 Peter Eisenman, The Staten Island Institute of Art and Science project, 1999 (concept diagram).

Source: Image courtesy of Eisenman Architects.

relationship between the roof-work and clothing anew? This last point flagships the essentiality of Semper's idea of theatricality for a critique of architecture's contemporaneity.

Contemporary criticism should consider Semper's distinction between planar and linear motifs fundamental to any fabric. According to him, "the cover's purpose is the opposite to that of binding... If the basic form of binding is linear, the surface appears as the formative element in everything intended to cover, protect, and close." He continues, "the most important general factor affecting the style of cover are the attributes of the surface; that is the extension in breadth and length, the absence of the third dimension..."[80] The distinction between the linear and planar motifs is crucial for understanding Semper's differentiation between the tectonic potentialities of Renaissance architecture from that of Gothic. It also offers a theoretical paradigm to discuss current architecture's turn to the surface. Technically, what is involved in the "turn" is that in the architecture of blob and fold, the grid and the linear dimension of the frame structure are treated as a surrogate for the wall, the covering element. This entails the critical position sectional investigation occupies in the design of playful surfaces. The phenomenon was not new. According to Rafael Moneo, the section is central to understanding the best work of James Sterling. According to him, in Leicester, (the section) is also the envelope, the skin.

Against the neutral, inert wall of traditional buildings, the modern architect discovered the lure of manipulating surfaces.[81] Since then, the element of clothing is contemplated as a thin membrane, the exterior face of which is embellished (tattooed) in its own right but also independent of the frame structure behind (Herzog & de

Meuron, Eberswalde Technical School Library, 1994). When the surface is reduced to an all-encompassing unified enclosure, the seam,
"the principle making a virtue out of necessity," vanishes.[82] In the
present rush to digital surface, the latter is treated like a carpet with
a significant difference; contrary to the fabric of a carpet, the digital surface disguises the grid of its fabric, most often on both sides.
Thus, the inevitable dismantling of the tectonic rapport between the
roof and the structural frame, proposing an alternative dressing to
re-present that relation.

When the surface is turned into the structure of ornament, then
the organic rapport between the art-form and ornamentation is not
bound by the "principle of surface dressing that makes it impossible to consider them separately."[83] Accordingly, "digital tectonics" is primarily informed by the structural-technical dimension
of the tectonic and aesthetic sensibilities permeating the present
spectacle culture. At a different level of consideration, I argue that
parametric alternatives suggest a structural organism analogous to
the global corporate organization where complexity is not achieved
through the resolution of contradictions but pliancy. As noted earlier, the blob represents a totalized system, leaving no space outside its surface. From this point of view, it is convincing to argue
that digitally fabricated forms do not maintain a critical position
against the ideological rapport between architecture and the cultural logic of late capitalism, to recall Fredric Jameson. Thanks to
digital reproductive techniques, the new materials produced by the
construction industry elevate the free-façade to a higher level of
autonomy. In addition to lightness, the digitally fabricated surface
is fluid, not much regarding the structural skeleton but to showcase
the commodity hallow as a film covering its skin. We are far from
the principle of thickening the wall and the principle of dressing
and the skin and bone architecture that attained tectonics in Mies's
Seagram building. We are also beyond the first-degree commodity fetishism, the separation between the act of producing and the
product to follow Arantes Pedro Fiori, for whom the fetishism in the
society of the spectacle (G. Dubord) "is a form of autonomization
of property and its representation."[84] The return of autonomous
surface to the main scene of contemporary architecture, however,
is beneficial: it brings to light Semper's theory of dressing. It provides unmediated access to the essentiality of roofing and clothing
and theatricality in contradistinction to theatricalization despite
or because of architecture's entanglement with the aesthetic of the
commodity form.

Notes

1 Gottfried Semper, *Style in Technical and Tectonic Arts; or Practical Aesthetics* (Santa Monica: The Getty Center, 2004), 243.
2 See Mark Wigley's contribution to the subject in *White Walls, Dresses: The Fashioning of Modern Architecture* (Cambridge: The MIT Press, 1995).
3 Le Corbusier, *The Decorative Art Today* (Cambridge: The MIT Press, 1987), 189.
4 Alina Payne, "The Sculpture-Architect's Drawing and Exchange between Arts," in Michael W. Cole, ed. *Sculptors' Drawings from Renaissance Italy* (London: Paul Holberton Publishing, 2014), 65.
5 See Gevork Hartoonian, "On Baroque," in *Time, History, and Architecture: Essays on Critical Historiography* (London: Routledge, 2018), 66–90.
6 Alina Payne, "Living Stones, Crying Walls: The Dangers of Enlivenment in Architecture from Renaissance to Warburg's Nachleben" in the Secret Lives of Artworks (Chicago: The University of Chicago Press, 2013), 328.
7 Gevork Hartoonian, "Back to Roofing and Wrapping," in *Architecture and Spectacle: A Critique* (London: Routledge, 2012), 241–251.
8 Alina Payne, "Beyond Kunstwollen: Alois Riegl and the Baroque," 2010, 21.
9 Walter Benjamin, *The Origin of German Tragic Drama*, 1985, 99.
10 Alois Riegl, *The Origins of Baroque Art in Rome*, 2010, 124.
11 Joseph Rykwert, *The Dancing Column: On Order in Architecture* (Cambridge: The MIT Press, 1996).
12 James S. Ackerman, *The Architecture of Michelangelo* (Chicago: The University of Chicago, 1986), 40.
13 Leon Battista Alberti, *On the Art of Building in Ten Book*, Susan E. Bassnett, trans. (New York: Braziller, 1969), 7. Gottfried Semper, *The Four Elements of Architecture and Other Essays*, trans. by Harry Francis Mallgrave & Wolfgang Herrmann (New York: Cambridge University Press, 1989).
14 Alois Riegl, *The Origins of Baroque Art in Rome*, 2010, 138.
15 See Hubert Damisch, "Compositing With Painting," in *Noah'a Ark: Essays on Architecture* (Cambridge: The MIT Press, 2016), 65–73.
16 Alois Riegl, *The Origins of Baroque Art in Rome*, 2010, 156.
17 Alina Payne, 2014, 68.
18 Alina Payne, 2014, 70.
19 On this subject, see Kenneth Frampton, *Studies in Tectonic Culture* (Cambridge: The MIT Press, 1995), 235.
20 Spyros Papapetros, *On the Animation of the Inorganic: Art, Architecture, and the Extension of Life* (Chicago: University of Chicago Press, 2012), 1–30.
21 Gevork Hartoonian, *Architecture and Spectacle: A Critique* (London: Routledge, 2016–12).
22 Gorrfired Semper, 221–225.
23 See Jose Miguel Mantilla, "Untangling the Threads of Gottfried Semper's Legacy in Le Corbusier's Formative Years," *Journal of Architectural Historians* 79, no. 2 (June 2020), 192–201.
24 Quoted in Margaret Olin, *Forms of Representation in Alois Riegl's Theory of Art* (University Park: The Pennsylvania State University Press, 1992), 52.
25 Gottfried Semper, *The Four Elements of Architecture and Other Essays*, trans. by Harry Francis Mallgrave & Wolfgang Herrmann (New York: Cambridge University Press, 1989), 269.

26 Le Corbusier, *Journey to the East* (Cambridge: The MIT Press, 1987), 60.

27 Mark Wigley, 1995, 5.

28 In the 2007 Getty Center translation, Le Corbusier's book is titled, *Toward an Architecture* in contrast to previous translations which occurs as *Towards a New Architecture*.

29 See Alina Payne, "The Sculpture-Architect's Drawing and Exchanges Between the Arts," in Michel Cole, ed. *Sculpture Drawings from Renaissance Italy* (Boston MA: Isabella Gardner Museum, 2014), 57–73.

30 Roberto Gargiani and Anna Rosellini, *Beton Brut and Ineffable Space, 1945–1965: Surface Materials and Psychophysiology of Vision* (Lausanne: EPFL Press, 2011), 129.

31 Gottfried Semper, *The Four Elements of Architecture and Other Essays*, trans. Harry Francis Mallgrave & Wolfgang Herrmann (New York: Cambridge University Press, 1989), 63.

32 Margaret Olin, *Forms of Representation in Alois Riegl's Theory of Art* (University Park: The Pennsylvania State University Press, 1992), 138.

33 Le Corbusier, *The Decorative Arts Today* (Cambridge: The MIT Press, 1987), 189.

34 Le Corbusier, *Journey to the East* (Cambridge: The MIT Press, 1987).

35 Le Corbusier, *The Decorative Arts Today*, 1987, 190.

36 Mark Wigley, 1995, 198.

37 Arantes Pedro Fiori, *The Forms of Rent: Architecture and Labor in the Digital Age* (Minneapolis: The University of Minnesota Press, 2019), 135.

38 Among other references, also see Christopher Long, "The Origins and Context of Adolf Loos's 'Ornament and Crime,'" *The Journal of Society of Architectural Historians*, vol. 68 no. 2 (June 2009), 200–223.

39 On Adolf Loos' various writing on garment and other design issues, see Adolf Opel, *Adolf Loos: Ornament and Crime, Selected Essays* (California: Ariadne Press, 1998).

40 See Max Risselada, ed. *Raumplan Versus Plan Libre* (Rotterdam: 010, 2008), originally published in 1987.

41 I am thinking of Henri Lefebvre, but also a host of other thinkers including Georg Simmel, Siegfried Kracauer, Martin Heidegger, and especially Walter Benjamin's reflections on everyday life. For a comprehensive discussion of the mentioned authors' views on everyday life, see Hartoonian (2000).

42 Gottfried Semper, *Style in Technical and Tectonic Arts; or Practical Aesthetics* (Santa Monica: The Getty Center, 2004), 113.

43 Gottfried Semper, 2004, 237–238.

44 The suggested differentiation was first introduced in the final chapter of Gevork Hartoonian, *Ontology of Construction* (Cambridge: Cambridge University Press, 1994), 81–90. (1994a). For the architectonic implication of dressing and "dressed-up," see Gevork Hartoonian, "The Fabric of Fabrication," *Textile: The Journal of Cloth & Culture* (2006): 270–291.

45 I am paraphrasing Harry Mallgrave's text, "Introduction" in Harry Francis Mallgrave, ed. *Otto Wagner* (Los Angeles: The Getty Center Publication Programs, 1993).

46 Margaret Olin, *Forms of Representation in Alois Riegl's Theory of Art* (University Park: The Pennsylvania State University Press, 1992), 124.

47 Bernard Cache, "Digital Semper," in Cynthia Davidson, ed. *Anymore* (Cambridge: The MIT Press, 2000), 190–197.

48 Harry F. Mallgrave, *Gottfried Semper: Architect of the Nineteenth Century* (New Haven: Yale University Press, 1996), 180.

49 Mario Carpo, ed. *The Digital Turn in Architecture: 1992-2012* (London: John Wiley & Sons Ltd, 2013), 146. In addition to this book, I have also consulted with Carpo, *The Second Digital Turn: Design beyond Intelligence* (Cambridge: The MIT Press, 2017).

50 Gottfried Semper, *The Four Elements of Architecture and Other Writings*, trans. H.F. Mallgrave & W. Hermann (New York: Cambridge University Press, 1989).

51 For a concise summary of the suggested development, see Mallgrave (1988).

52 Gottfried Semper, 2004, 247.

53 Gottfried Semper, 2004, 268.

54 Here I am benefiting from Mallgrave (1996: 293).

55 Quoted in Scott Wolf, *Karl Fredrich Schinkel: The Tectonic Unconscious and New Science of Subjectivity*, 1997, unpublished dissertation, UMI Dissertation Service.

56 Otto Wagner, Sketches, Projects and Executed Buildings, trans. Peter Haiko (New York: Rizzoli International Publication Co., 1987), 8. For the theme of theatricality in French realist painting of the early nineteenth century, see Michael Fried, Courbet's Realism (Chicago: Chicago University Press, 1990).

57 Otto Wagner, Sketches, Projects and Executed Buildings, 1987, 10.

58 Mohsen Mostafavi and David Leatherbarrow, *On Weathering: The Life of Buildings in Time* (Cambridge: The MIT Press, 1993), 59.

59 Gottfried Semper, 2004, 438–439.

60 See Gevork Hartoonian, *Crisis of the Object: The Architecture of Theatricality* (London: Routledge, 2006), chapter 4.

61 Harry F. Mallgrave, *Gottfried Semper: Architect of the Nineteenth Century* (New Haven: Yale University Press, 1996), 355–381.

62 Jose Miguel Mantilla, *Journal of the Society of Architectural Historians*, vol. 97, no. 2 (June 2020): 198.

63 Benjamin Binstock, "Forward," in Alois Riegl, ed. *Historical Grammar of the Visual Arts* (New York: Zone Books, 2004), 14–16.

64 Peter Osborne, *The Politics of Time: Modernity and Avant-Grade* (New York: Verso, 1995), 14–16.

65 Walter Benjamin quoted in Peter Osborne, 1995, 184.

66 See Antoine Picon, *Digital Culture in Architecture* (Basel: Birkhauser, 2010), specially "Experiments in Form and Performance," 59–114.

67 The following section benefits from the author's *Architecture and Spectacle: A Critique* (London: Routledge, 2016).

68 Joseph Rykwert, "Organic and Mechanic," *RES: Journal of Anthropology and Aesthetics* 22 (Autumn 1992): 11–18.

69 Caroline van Eck, *Organicism in Nineteenth-Century Architecture* (Amsterdam: A & N Press, 1994), 19.

70 Here and in the following, I am benefiting from Gottfried Semper's ideas discussed in his text on Style, 2004, 345.

71 For other examples, see Mario Carpo, footnote # 41.

72 Anthony Vidler, *Wrapped Space: Art, Architecture, and Anxiety in Modern Culture* (Cambridge: The MIT Press, 2000), 227.

73 Lars Spuybroek, *The Sympathy of Things: Ruskin and the Ecology of Design* (Rotterdam: NAi Publishers, 2011), 31. The entire chapter "The Digital Nature of Gothic" is suggested.
74 Lars Spuybroek, *The Sympathy of Things*, 2011, 66.
75 Horst Bredekamp, *The Lure of Antiquity and the Cult of Machine* (Princeton: Markus Wiener Publishers, 1995), 49.
76 Gevork Hartoonian, *Architecture and the Spectacle*, 2016–12.
77 Rosalind Krauss, *The Originality of the Avant-Garde and Other Modernist Myth* (Cambridge: The MIT Press, 1985), 54. Her positions should be read against the background of Clement Greenberg, who saw flatness as a theme working towards a criticism of modernism developed from the inside. On this subject, see Leo Steinberg in the following footnote.
78 Leo Steinberg, *Other Criteria: Confrontation with Twentieth-Century Art* (New York: Oxford University Press, 1972), 1972–1990.
79 On this subject, see Hartoonian (1994b: 68–80).
80 Gottfried Semper, *Style in Technical and Tectonic Arts*, 2004, 123.
81 Rafael Moneo, *Theoretical Anxiety and Design Strategies in the Work of Eight Contemporary Architects* (Cambridge: The MIT Press, 2004), 23.
82 Gottfried Semper, *Style in Technical and Tectonic Arts*, 2004, 154.
83 Gottfried Semper, *Style in Technical and Tectonic Arts*, 2004, 246.
84 Arantes Pedro Fiori, *The Forms of Rent*, 2019, 73.

4 On Labor

Back to Work![1]

At no point in contemporary history have the complexities involved in the production of architecture seemed as transparent as they do today. Dialectically, I should add that never before has architectural ideology operated as sophistically as experienced in the *silence* overshadowing the profound need for an historico-theoretical criticism of architecture's contemporaneity. From Filippo Brunelleschi's design for the dome of the Cathedral of Santa Maria de Fiore to many modernists' assumption that architecture expresses its *Zeitgeist*; to Peter Eisenman's theorization of architecture (and the reader might want to add other architects with their relevant contributions to my shortlist), today we are witnessing the increasing domination of architecture by a production and consumption system that has culminated in global capitalism. This historical phenomenon has been openly and sometimes diligently, rather than critically, unpacked, discussed in scholarly publications and the daily newspapers of cosmopolitan cities worldwide. If during the early decades of the last century, technology and machine products were considered comrades to the historical avant-garde's project to close the schism between the abstract and autonomous architecture of modernism and the everyday life of its citizens, by contrast, now, architecture is contemplated and experienced as the ultimate commodity-image while sheltering the broad spectrum of the products of the present media-driven consumer culture. Gone in this process of instrumentalization are those aspects of modernism—the project of social housing, for instance—where the processes and the idea of providing affordable and decent living space for the masses (middle and lower classes) did indeed correspond to the ontological aspects of architecture; that is, constructing the conditions of life. Thus, the urgent need to re-think the collective

DOI: 10.4324/9781003360445-5

dimension of architecture in the context of a global mass production and consumption system, digitally disseminated images, and virtually controlled public spaces.

Throughout history, many trades and industries have been involved in the production of architecture. Indeed, the chaos experienced at the construction site is because of coming and going and the replacement of one group of skilled and non-skilled laborers with another. Even though the industrialization of materials, techniques, and skills has distanced the art of building from its craft-based tradition, the collective is still operative in the production of architecture. In addition to its appropriation by the masses, what makes the film—the most *modern* artistry—a good analog for architecture, is the centrality of montage and tectonics to these two industries. Call it the *common*: montage in film and tectonics in architecture operate like a double agent. Meaning that what is *internal* to architecture and film paradoxically weaves these two artworks into the *totality*, the operative engine of capitalism. Central to tectonics is the transgression of construction, charging the constructed form with excess, licensing architecture to enter the prevailing cultural domain. In this, but also in the preparation of the site, the transformation of material to materiality, and the embellishment of the constructed form with proper dressing and relevant detailing, the tectonic might plunge architecture further into the instrumental logic of capitalism and the prevailing commodity fetishism. Such is the relationship between architecture and capitalism today: a gridlock, indeed, if we put aside the appeal to theory at work since the 1970s as a remedy for the crisis of architecture.

There are two interrelated points in the rhetorical title of my proposed call. The first concerns the invisible nature of labor in getting from here to somewhere, both physically and mentally. Space is thus opened, and separation occurs as a measure of the dialectics of labor and time. Related to this is the dual nature of labor that culminates in the final form of any product and architecture in particular. Giorgio Agamben writes that the double nature of labor "presents us now with one face now with another, without making both visible in the same instance."[2] It constitutes the spectral dimension of the aesthetic of the fetishism of commodities. In the age of similitude (M. Foucault), cultural products were embellished to be part of a more considerable *distance* that separated the human world from the natural world, the Benjaminian world of aura. The space resultant from the object's departure from the age of similitude is given to commodity form, the modus operandi of the suppressed use-value. The appearance of most products in modernity (the aesthetic replacement of the

classical mimesis with the Marxian concept of fetishism) *looks* autonomous enough to be considered a temporal monad independent of
the consumed labor. In this mutation, what is hard to neglect is the
well-coordinated dialectics of time and labor that permeate the architecture's production processes, from the early goofy design sketches
to the completion and embellishment of construction.

This chapter's title concerns the particularity of that which has
convincingly proven that architectural theory has been in crisis for
some time. There are several reasons for this, among which I would
like to highlight in passing the coincidence between the death of
Jacque Derrida with the second surge in digital reproducibility that
took place at the turn of this century. This unfolding has disarmed
architects and critics of any substantial theorization of architecture
except re-thinking a host of already examined concepts of the past
along with if not aftermath of natural and social disasters; from flood
to sustainability, pandemic, and whatever might come next. Derrida's
death was symptomatic of both the end of Theory and architecture's
turn to philosophical discourses that started roughly with Louis
Kahn and other architects' theorization of architecture alongside
intuitive interpretations of existentialism and phenomenology, end-
ing with the Museum of Modern Art's exhibition of "Deconstructivist
Architecture," 1988. From existentialism to deconstruction, the clos-
ing circle was not the central concern of architecture; it was rather
internal to philosophy. The architecture was indeed an unwanted
guest in the "circle." Thanks to digital reproducibility, architecture's
agency is now (similar to the nineteenth century) tossed back to the
realm of technology with several consequences, as discussed in previous chapters and in the following pages.

Since the nineteenth century, architecture has struggled to achieve
autonomy, formal, or tectonic, while tuning the culture of building
with the latest technical advancements. Whereas the shortcomings of
formal autonomy should be associated with the genesis of the bourgeoisie, Gottfried Semper's theorization of tectonics foregrounded a
semi-autonomous architecture. Considering Ernst Bloch's notion of
non-simultaneity, it is not farfetched to claim that Semper's theorization of architecture foreshadowed the uneven rapport between labor
and temporality. This dimension of Semper's theory is less-discussed
in the available English literature, and I wish to take full benefit of it
for the argument presented here.

This chapter will discuss the complex rapport between architecture and temporality in conjunction with two Marxian prejudices.
That temporality is not a choice but an attribute of a particular stage

of production, distribution, and consumption of commodities, architecture included. Secondly, a critical analysis of temporality and labor in architecture necessitates an historico-theoretical project that should depart from the present state of architectural praxis. But what would be the index of a critical departure from the prevailing state of affairs when digitalization has fundamentally changed the design process? Like a technical operator, most architects today design while silently communicating with a pre-programmed machine, the mechanism of which enforces more limits than offering diverse arrays of conceptual compositions. I argue that the speed involved in parametric design and the variety of reproduced forms are the two sides of commodity form disseminated across all cultural products of the present finance capitalism.

Attending selective episodes of the technification of architecture,[3] I argue that architects, critics, and historians should focus on saving the historicity of the art of building, the tectonics in particular. This is vital at this point in history when everything, including the logic and processes of instrumentalization, is coated with the aesthetic of commodity form. In overcoming the present one-dimensional indulgence with parametric, "universal architecture," the tectonics should draw from the uneven interplay of contingent forces that, interestingly enough, are sediments of historical progress orchestrated by the instrumentalization of technology. While highlighting tectonics, it's not my intention to discuss labor and time economics. Like the two-stage transformation of spectacle, as noted in the previous chapter, I wish to demonstrate that in digital reproducibility, the invisibility of labor is further obscured, and the spectral nature of the aesthetic of fetishism has heightened at the expense of detailing.

From Four Seasons to Four Industries

In his 1910 essay, "Architecture," Adolf Loos emulated an imaginary vernacular milieu wherein objects and names would mirror each other, the aura of which was disrupted by a villa, an architect's design. Juxtaposing the villa's pretentious presence with the vernacular abode with a roof signifying nothing but "roof," it's tempting to think whether Loos had read Alois Riegl. The architect's description of the imaginary scenic landscape recalls Riegl's report of what he saw settling at the top of Alpine peaks. Reiterating the replacement of haptic with optic, Riegl wrote (1899) that what the soul of modern man craves is "this presentment of order and legitimacy over chaos, of harmonious over dissonance, of the rest over the movement that we call mood [*Stimmung*]. Its elements are restfulness and far-sightedness [*Fernsicht*]."⁴ This is not a far-fetched association considering Loos's advocacy for sensation, one of the primary tasks of a well-dressed building. Picking on the villa, Loos wanted to expose the weak side of modernism that, when writing his essay, had hugely invested in capturing the spirit of modern zeitgeist and technology at once. Loos's criticism of modernity turned out to be more relevant in the postmodern moment even though his competition entry for the Chicago Tribune tower was considered symptomatic of postmodern architecture; a model displayed in the exhibition *The Presence of the Past*, Venice, 1980.

Loos's untimely competition entry presented an alternative to schemes that tried inventing new forms borrowing from architecture's past treasures. Loos's Dorian column wanted to impose "order" on a city that was thwarted by the profit-making plans of the rising urban developers. Paradoxically and given his imaginary villa, Loos's entry injected a dissonance into the harmony planners desired to impose on the city of Chicago. A Doric column with a shaft reaching a 21-story building, it "was to be a pure classic form, classic and therefore outside the reach of fashion, ..." wrote Joseph Rykwert.⁵ Still, considering the detached position of the contemporary needle-like tall buildings, we should agree with Hubert Damisch, for whom the column has a double finality, to the need to and to autonomy. He wrote, "As a sign, the column provides proof, in its very appearance, of the labor at stake in it: a labor in which arbitrariness and necessity constantly exchange masks, a labor that plays at will with all of the motivations from which its form emerges."⁶ This brilliant reflection on classical Orders applies to Loos's competition column entry but also the digitally morphed tall buildings, the surface of which masks labor and materiality in contrast to the abstract textile-like woven skin of Mies's Seagram building.

A self-designated Roman architect, Loos positioned himself in the reverse order of the historical timeline, enabling himself to see modernity as an accomplished project. This reversed perspectival cannon allowed Loos to consider himself an architect armed with skills to recollect a handful of techniques from the bygone traditions of building art. However, he did take it upon himself to deconstruct the modernist vanguard obsession with the new and the architect's technologically empowered subjectivity. Hal Foster writes, "Far from the transcendence of death, this loss of finitude is a death-in-itself, as figured in the ultimate trope of indistinction, living 'with one's corpse.'"⁷ Epitomized in the tomb, eternal solitude from the living and historical constraints was, for Loos, paradoxically, one of the two typologies worthy of the name "architecture." The other was the monument. Interestingly enough, these two building types are symptomatic of the invisibility of labor in architecture for reasons elucidated below.

Loos's rapport with tradition was neither nostalgic nor regressive. His tendency to use particular materials for the cladding of interior and exterior surfaces was indeed part of a process of recollection of images that were not abstract but indexed with labor, time, and materiality. Using semi-precious materials on walls and ceilings, Loos avoided framing them as his contemporaries did. But always "integral, continuous surfaces, always as plain as possible, always displaying their proper texture: almost as if they were a kind of ornament, an ornament which showed the pleasure providence took in making them, as the more obvious type of ornament would display the pleasure experienced by his fellow-men."[8] I will come back to the topic of ornament below, but for now, we should focus on the distinction Loos made and the emphasis he put on the interior spaces of residential buildings. And this, in contradistinction to the prevailing urban environment, was to recode the feeling of being at home as rooted in vernacular and aside from the bourgeois kinship with *objects*. These existential feelings, often mixed with the architect's responses to hostile climatic conditions such as sun, wind, and snow, were at the same time conjured with a particular experience of labor and materiality, stone, wood, plaster, mirror, and carpet. In many ways, the regional character and four seasons were essential for architecture's realization in pre-modern times. Climatic conditions were decisive for timetabling the coming and going of trades involved in the construction process. This coordinated labor system lasted even until the middle of the last century. Even the contemporary lineup of various trades in the construction site had inherited aspects of the past when industrial techniques did not mediate climatic conditions. They were instead invented primarily to transform most of the, so to speak, wet construction systems into dry ones. It was also aimed to decrease and replace labor-intensive skills with pre-manufactured machine products.

Loos's empathy with the interiority of the dwelling had no choice but to stand up to the technification of architecture that had attained more visibility in the late 1920s. At the time and in the background of the 1914 Werkbund debate, it was clear that sooner or later, the artisanal forms of products would be replaced by a different sense of objectivity, less intimate and more abstract.[9] I do not intend to present a detailed account of this historical transformation. Instead, in highlighting important and relevant *dots* in the history of modern architecture, I wanted to show that abstraction in architecture was an inevitable outcome of the overwhelming presence of the aesthetic of commodity form and the de-skilling of the construction site labor into robotic activities. Thus, Le Corbusier's plan libre soon deconstructed the traditional notion of room and the Loosian sense of interiority implicit in the idea of Raum-plan (space-plan). These two planimetric organizations were reconsidered on the occasion of the rise of existentialism in the post-war era in Louis Kahn's conceptualization of *room*. Sympathetic to Romanesque architecture, Kahn turned the primary category of the room into a generic type using it repetitively for diverse purposes, from a house to any large-scale public building, even into the city. Architecture for Khan was a constellation of rooms (Dhaka) allegorically denoting a "name," the building's primary purpose.[10] His was a mystical association between "naming" and the building's purpose.

The concept of repetition and its various architectonic manifestations permeating Kahn's work was in Mies van der Rohe's later work decoded as *beinahe nichts*, or "almost nothing." Whereas repetition in Kahn's architecture was part of the postmodernist return to premodern building typologies, for Mies, it was a strategy to resist the early modernist tendency for the "new." However, Mies's architecture was agile to approximate the past, decoding the tectonic image inherent in Greek temples. In doing so, he changed history retroactively, "not the actual past but the balance between actuality and virtuality in the past."[11] In deconstructing the room's enclosed interiority, Mies juxtaposed the transparency of the glass enclosure with the fabric of the curtain behind to denote the u-form of the room, a space covered by four carpets, as Loos speculated on the origin of architecture. In the Barcelona Pavilion, Hubert Damisch writes, "no wall is pierced by holes, where the passage of bodies and light is reduced to a play of intervals and transparencies."[12] The Miesian "more is less" suggests reducing a phenomenon into its smallest atomic unit, the void implicit in the work of Samuel Beckett, which according to Fredric Jameson, "are always haunted by the dearest bourgeois domestic memories,"[13] and artifacts shaped and refined by the artisanal touch of the hand. And yet again, Mies's later architecture unleashed the "modernity" of the thing, one half of which, Baudelaire said, is ephemeral. The other half takes us back to the ur-form of architecture, the tectonics of the Greek temple. Paradoxically, I would argue that the Miesian void undermined the modernist temporality represented in the overwhelming importance of circulation in Le Corbusier's planimetric and sectional organization. Le Corbusier's creative deconstruction of the enclosed form of the bourgeois room, its inwardness, and the "restriction of human existence to a private sphere free from the power of reification. Yet as a private sphere, it belongs ... to the social structure."[14] In the same text, Jameson reminds us of the significance of rooms for Benjamin. He compares the German thinker's Arcades project, a collection of outlines, with the city as a collection of rooms, the idea Kahn would have liked to emulate.

At this point, and in the manner of Jameson, we should contemplate "the non-temporality of repetition." This means repetition is a desirable strategy to suspend, if not postpone, labor's disappearance as use-value is transformed into exchange-value.[15] Accordingly, I want to argue that both Kahn and Mies used the strategy of repetition toward two different ends and temporal connotations. In Kahn's work, repetition aimed at re-territorializing the classical syntax re-coded by the French Revolutionary architects. In a nutshell, the repetition for the American architect meant "time without future," a Miesian almost nothing! The Miesian repetition was a reminder of the mechanization processes and the repetitive nature of work.

Here, and in regard to Kahn's notion of monumentality, we should be reminded that, similar to most cultural products, monuments of the past have been apprehended as part of cultural heritage, disregarding their production process, the invested labor, and craftsmanship. It is appropriate here to introduce Peter Weiss and his writing on the Pergamon Altar in *Aesthetic of Resistance*. Following Benjamin, Weiss investigated subjectivities beyond their immediacies, shifting the focus of interpretation to the situation of the production of the work. According to Fredric J. Schwartz, Weiss imagined "slaves and captives hauling blocks of marble for the construction of the altar, and the artists (whom he positions with absolute precision between labor and power) sketching them in delight, sublimating oppression into art."[16] There is nothing new about architecture's allegiance to power; what should be recognized is the architect's position within the given power structure, to follow Benjamin in "The Author as Producer." For instance, Kahn's use of historical typologies wrapped in brick was a further digression from the invisibility of labor at the expense of materiality and form.

On the other hand, Mies de-territorialized "intimate" received architectonics to illuminate detailing wherein diverse materiality and labor are in action. He pushed this to the point that the alleged nihilism he would evoke coincided analogically with the incompleteness of the final result of the labor wherein the exchange value overrides the use value.[17] Synchronic with the state of culture in late capitalism, Mies' late work was antithetical to the post-war tendency for "image building." The postmodernist entertainment of image was to blur the line separating architecture from pop art. In *Complexity and Contradiction in Architecture* (1966), Robert Venturi had already facilitated the intrusion of pop culture into architecture; Mies's turn to the tectonics instead embraced the ethos of modernism to be pursued by many contemporary architects, Renzo Piano, for one. As for the technification of architecture, it seems that Loos was aware of the inevitable impact of industrialization on the construction process. He differed from both Kahn and Mies because he could not but emulate this historical opening in analogy to Gottfried Semper's archaeology of four industries. In consolidating his proposed four elements of architecture, Semper's theory casts a new light on the notion of room, shaking the empowerment of natural categories such as wet and dry, four seasons, and the eternal return of the same.

In his famous text, *The Four Elements of Architecture*,[18] Semper proposed that architecture evolved using elements drawn from the products of four industries. He went further, noting that the skills and motifs characteristic of the hearth, the terrace, the roof, and the enclosure of the Caribbean hut, displayed at the Great Exhibition of London (1851), stemmed from stylistic transformations developed in ceramics, masonry, carpentry, and textiles industries respectively. Accordingly, Semper mapped architectural knowledge in two primordial aspects of dwelling, namely the earthwork, the preparation of the site to receive the framework, and a detailed procedure (design?) that would result in the tectonic emulation of dualities such as heaviness and lightness, enclosure and exposure (nakedness). His anthropological esteem was further empowered when he compared the Caribbean hut with a reconstructed Maori village from New Zealand, also displayed in the Crystal Palace. Whereas the former model confirmed Semper's concept of tectonics formulated in analogy to the essentiality of the aforementioned four industries, the Maori village, by contrast, exemplified a civilization that "stopped at a very early time of its development," evident in products that fetishize textile motifs.[19] Witnessing the emerging industries at the dawn of modernization, Semper argued that almost every culture passes through the exigencies of the proposed four industries and that in their uneven developmental moments, each culture accumulates partial knowledge of them. He thus laid out a semi-unequal development of nations and a non-simultaneous cultural appreciation of what Koselleck spoke of "horizon of expectation."[20]

Semper's speculative observations foreshadowed the uneven dissemination of the cultural totality enacted by capitalism in western and non-western hemispheres at the dawn of mechanical reproducibility. In the Prolegomena to *Der Stil* (1863), he wrote:

> Capitalism certainly makes every effort to have the fine arts serve its ends, just as it borrows all its technical means from science. It has brought the division of labor (a practice understandably necessary for coping with the vast scale of an enterprise) but in a way that is highly detrimental to the hoped-for success. ... it separates the so-called ornamental from formal and technical aspects of art in a purely mechanical way, immediately betraying its lack of feeling for and misunderstanding of the true relationship between the various means the artist uses to produce his work.

In addition to the fact that different cultures attain diverse artistic achievements due to their historical and geographic contingencies, what is also implied in Semper's criticism of capitalism is the unequal development of the four industries in a given period. Herein lies the core of less discussed seeds of political economy in Semper's discourse that has been taken for his materialist tendency. This much is clear from Rykwert's reading of Semper's London lecture. Rykwert wrote that, in the presence of the Crystal Palace, Semper encountered "the hub of industrial civilization and the center of the empire, where the productions of outlandish and 'primitive' people were available not as rare curiosities he had seen in Dresden but as a mass of imports—this period so followed architecturally, proved very fruitful theoretically."[21] Semper's exposure to the phantasmagoria of Crystal Palace had two significant consequences. Firstly, the skills and labor contributing to the concrete conditions for the emergence and further development of the alleged four industries were integral to humanity's everyday life. Accordingly, the early stages of surplus *accumulation* were decisive for the historical departure from semi-animal conditions that heavily relied on nature and natural products. Secondly, while making an imaginary association between the elemental products of the four industries with the building art, Semper's theorization could not but operate primarily at the artistic level (the art-form), leaving labor and exchange value untouched. However, upon their transposition, the earlier elemental motifs foreshadowed skills, techniques, and labor which eventually constituted the core of trades constructive for the erection of a building during two long historical periods, the classical and the modern. Whereas the architectonics of one was primarily dictated by the masonry construction system's spatial and formal potentialities, modern architecture took full advantage of techniques working with the emerging steel and glass materials. Alternatively, a composite was sought, combining masonry and steel-frame construction systems. Herein lies the genesis of modern architects' heterogeneous approaches to the interior organization of architecture, from room to open-plan and Raum-plan and then back to the room, given the architects mentioned earlier.

Like most transactions in capitalism, the dialectics involved in exchange value supersede the use value; "a human purpose of the commodity in the moment of its direct relation of utility for a subject—is only the effect of the system of exchange value, a concept produced and developed by it."[22] Considered along these lines, the alleged materialist bone of Semper's theory was not farfetched after all! His was instead a naïve expression of traditional Marxist base-superstructure dependency better understood in Benjamin's following words; "it is not the economic origins of culture that will be presented, but the expression of the economy in its culture." And he continued, at issue is "the attempt to grasp an economic process as perceptible *Ur*-phenomenon, from out of which proceed all manifestations of life in the arcades."[23] Accordingly, the motives Semper enumerated were essential for demonstrating why the four industries were critical for advancing architecture in general and tectonics in particular. In hindsight, Semper was saying nothing but a Benjaminian appreciation of culture towards a critical understanding of the logic of the given economic system, labor, technique, and skills combined, which during the nineteenth century were not wholly emancipated from their expressive ur-forms. Nevertheless, "Labor specialization, rationalization, and integration of social functions created a techno-body of society,"[24] that had a profound impact on the sensorium system of the body, perception in particular, as individual experimentation with reality was transformed in tandem with the dissemination of mechanical reproducibility into the cultural realm.

Aestheticization of Labor

Whereas Semper sought the motifs produced by the four industries autonomous and transferable particles, by the establishment of the Bauhaus in 1919, objects were conceived and produced in full consideration of the transformability of technical into the cultural realm. Apropos, the work embellished by technical means introduced a sense of excess, an image independent of the purpose of the object, suggested in Benjamin's notion of phantasmagoria as part of the experience of the Crystal Palace exhibition. In *The Arcades Project*, Benjamin explores various aspects of the everyday life of nineteenth-century European culture and mapped the scope of the commodification of *things*. His project showcased the range of technological transformation and its infusion into the cultural realm as a "dialectical image," a historiographic notion central to Benjamin's philosophy of history. In exploring the world of commodities, Benjamin was equally interested in the seeds of resistance nested in ruins left by history's progress.

Interestingly enough, Benjamin recalled Semper's remarks on gas lighting to address the extension of commodification. The German architect wrote, "What a splendid invention this gaslighting is! How many ways has it not enriched the festive occasion of life (not to mention its infinite importance for our practical needs)!"[25] We will notice a similar enthusiasm Marx expressed about emerging new techniques.

Consequential to the technification of artwork was the expansion of the notion of total design beyond the Arts and Crafts movement's apprehension of labor to the point that design attained a state of semi-autonomy given the technical apparatus prevailing in the age of mechanical reproducibility. From "Realism" and *Sachlichkeit* to the New Objectivity (*Neue Sachlichkeit*) of the early last century, the idea of design could not but accommodate the final product to the aestheticization of the object (image) in excess and beyond its primary purpose. Reminding the reader of the dominant conventions of Weimar photography, Benjamin Buchloh has recently observed that one of a committed photographer's tasks was to side-track "the seduction of the New Objectivity," thus producing work different from both "Moholy-Nagy's technocratic specularity and Renger-Patzsch's melancholic affirmation of an unalterable universal reification, consequentially enacting fractography serial and procedural principles."[26] Christian Lodder also writes that even in the Russia of 1917–22, "there were important differences between Gabo's constructions with their rather mathematical approach to form and the more empathically textual, abstract work of Tatlin."[27] Vladimir Tatlin's constructivist reliefs, counter-reliefs, and numerous kiosks and stage-set designs were indeed inspired by pre-modern Russia's iconological traditions and a vision of primitivism that emphasized the texture of material (*faktura*), use of simple techniques, and disdain for "artistic design." Most European architects of the time were primarily trying to achieve various interpretations of the Corbusian Five Points of architecture at the expense of labor and skills involved in construction processes. Apropos, the argument that exceptional cases aside, modern architecture ensured architecture's autonomy from theoretical premises drawn from architecture's rapport with both "four seasons" and the Semperian four industries. The historicity of this unfolding which underpins various architectural tendencies until the rise of digital reproducibility, is the missing argument in most contemporary theorization and criticism of architecture, I believe.

However, there were moments in the modernism of the 1920s (both in the Soviets and affiliates of the Bauhaus, such as housing projects advanced by Ernst May and Richard Wagner) when the politics and tactics coincided with the ontological aspects of architecture that is, the construction of the conditions of life. The processes of thinking and designing as such were an aberration in the long history of capitalism. And yet, the same phenomenon was simultaneously integral to optimum forms conceived in correspondence to labor skills and construction techniques, which were in tandem with the *collective* dimension of architecture. I argue that the task of committed architects today is to explore the possibility of re-thinking "aberration" in the prevailing global system of mass production and consumption, digitally disseminated images, and virtually controlled public spaces.

Back to Work: Re-imagining Architectural Project

To consolidate the Five Points of Architecture, Le Corbusier scrapped the surface of architectonic elements of the Roman empire, showcasing aspirations for abstract platonic geometries. This was an effective strategy even though he failed to bring forth the anonymous labor of enslaved people and artisans who had built these marvels of history.[28] Discussing the impact of technology on auratic work (pre-modern artwork redundantly simplified), Benjamin wrote:

> To prey an object from its shell, to destroy its aura, is the mark of a perception whose "sense of the universal quality of things" has increased to such a degree that it extracts it even from a unique object by means of reproduction.[29]

Seemingly, Benjamin was concerned with the layers covering the thingness of the object in the age of mechanical reproducibility to the point that contemplation must either embrace alienation (to use an outdated term) or stick with available critical positions. Jameson expands this simplistic view of how things work in capitalism and suggests that, since the 1960s, the appearance of capitalism has changed thanks to the emergence of non-class agencies such as gender and race.[30] We can push his position further and agree that a hot topic such as sustainability in capitalism "is paradoxical, to say the least: it is a system based on the constant production of all kinds of inequalities—including unequal distribution of entropy, spreading hot and cold societies across the globe, making it also not so difficult to guess which of these thermodynamic poles feeds the other."[31] And yet, in history, and we can extend this to architectural history, categories of labor, "the intolerable spectacle of backbreaking millennial toil of millions of people from the earliest moments of history," when "women's work, the oldest form of the division of labor, quiet unavoidable, …," are, according to Jameson, the "nightmare of history."[32] Apropos, no right-minded person will deny the positive aspects of gender and race transformation. The same goes with the present turn to climate change and sustainability, each disclosing mediations on societal and technical status that have major impact on the division of labor. However, all of these occur within capitalism, a system in which capital and land are the most decisive factors towards realizing particular building types. Accordingly, should not a critical theorization of architecture today scrap down the surfaces of the digitally reproduced architecture to show what supports its undulating and multilayered surfaces? This proposition resonates Hal Foster's reading of Kerry James Marshall's painting, *Underpainting*, 2018, where he highlights the importance of history for critically assessing the present high-tech digital art and architecture.[33]

If, in the early decades of the last century, architectural projects invested one-dimensionally in the assimilation of the technical and aesthetic apparatus of modernization. How should we re-imagine architectural projects today, given the following two contemporary developments? Firstly, given the avant-garde failure to integrate art and architecture with life, modernity remains a monadic episode of human civilization, a singular spaceship floating around the globe serving regions with appropriate receptions. This much is evident from the diversity of architectural praxis realized after WWII and its current dissemination into contemporary non-western regions of the world despite or because of the absence of the agency of the historical avant-garde. Secondly, we have accepted that modern architecture unfolding in the western hemisphere was only one of the constellations of "singular modernity," coined by Jameson. The dialectical image implied in these two tires of our contemporary history demands discussing architecture and time beyond stylistic and historicist stories. We need to dissect contemporary architecture from top to bottom back and forth to show that "Theory, which once eagerly fed on the artistic gratification of a sense perception altered by technology has itself become a purely aesthetic and consumerist process."[34] Correspondence to this is the well-known fact among architects that the time spent on documentation and construction of a project overrides the time allocated for the design process. This is a typical trajectory permeating the organization of most commodities. The key player in this ratio is the phantom of labor cost, the central focus of most technical innovations in modern times. While after World War II, architects could produce institutional work using mixed intensive hand-machine techniques and labor. By the shift from mechanical to digital reproducibility, the final work, in most cases, is less "subjective" (the inner world of an architect) but technical and in coordination with the production process, and the developer's financial greed. The architectural qualities are now "assessed according to their visual impact, reinforcing the importance of the appearance of skin and surface."[35] The accumulative nature of the aestheticization of architecture in both ages of mechanical and digital reproducibility, interestingly enough, corresponds to the accumulated wealth by 1% of the world population of the rich in contradistinction to the 99% of the lower ladder of socio-economics of most contemporary democracies. This might be one reason why significant investment has been channeled during the last two decades to building typologies financed by major corporate institutions, from high-rise corporate towers to museums, opera houses, and, lately, athletic stadiums. Like famous commodity brands, and thanks to advanced photographic techniques, these building types are consumed not as civic but as images promoting further touristic appreciation of architecture, Benjamin notices in The Work of Art Essay as early as 1935. Architecture today is empowered by an image from its inception to completion and into its touristic appropriation.

The above analogy makes further sense if considered alongside Jameson's brilliant essay, "Time and the Concept of Modernity."[36] Recalling Derrida saying that "it's always too late to talk about time," Jameson claims that "the juxtaposition of time and architecture" proves otherwise. He writes, "For here, perhaps, it is precise that buried temporal presupposition which it is a question of paradoxically bringing to light and revealing or unveiling: the deeper temporal structure of what seems absolutely spatial and at the antipodes of a temporal art like music or poetry." He continues, "It would be useful to have not merely an inventory of the architectural, but above all, a chronicle of moments in which architectural theories have found themselves obliged to raise the subject in the first place."[37] Such are historical dots that this chapter has frequently tried to make short stops, and such is the fact that throughout history, many trades and industries, each with particular timelines, were involved in the production of architecture. This much is also clear from the chaos experienced on the construction site, the coming and going of one group of skilled and non-skilled laborers with another. Alvaro Siza's experience speaks for itself:

> As is almost always the case, there are numerous problems when several companies are involved in construction works due to inter-coordination difficulties, sometimes protracting the work excessively. There are often long intervals after one stage has come and end until the decision for the accomplishment of the next has been made.[38]

Imagining the construction site as a theatrical stage, Siza sees the pauses made in the preparation and completion of each stage of construction as an opportunity for the involved trades and even the client (in small-scale projects) to exchange ideas. Even though the teamwork nature of architecture is not limited to the design process and continues to the construction site, one cannot but agree with Wilfried Wang's fifth interrelated point that aligns architecture with the capitalistic structure of an optimized business. He writes, "the increased division of labor that has resulted in architect no longer being in charge of every aspect of the building, although they may still determine the building's typology and its envelop,"[39] a state of design enforced by the shift from paper to digital media tools. The architect has also lost the degree of imagination Siza enjoys scribbling on paper when even making a conversation.

Even though the industrialization of materials, techniques, and skills has distanced the art of building from its craft-based tradition mentioned earlier, what is still operative in the production of architecture is *collective*. With this in mind, it's not far fetching to say that what makes architecture exceptional among other cultural products is its *presence*; nevertheless, in most cases, architecture not only hides the labor involved in transforming materials into materiality (in the Semperian sense), but it also covers its internal organization tangible in the preparatory design drawings. Whereas aspects of tectonics attain visibility after the completion of construction, the internal organization of a building, its life-form as worked out in the plan and section drawings remains buried behind an image that most often certifies architecture's belonging to the aesthetic imaginary experienced across all products of contemporary mass culture. Benjamin seemingly was aware of the invisibility of the plan and the inadequacy of words to explain the sublimity of the Baroque. He wrote, "In the ruins of great buildings, the idea of the plan speaks more impressively than in lesser buildings, however well preserved they are."[40] In the Work of Art essay, he rejected the "touristic" experience of architecture, highlighting the essentiality of distraction for the experience of architecture, as is the case with the cinematic experience. Despite the invisibility of labor and plan, architecture's material and spatial presence stands out under the sun, moon, and in the city while superseding artistic autonomy on behalf of becoming a constructive player in the construction of the conditions of life.

Highlighting issues stated in previous pages, it is appropriate now to ask what does it concern the labor question. The question does not concern labor as such, an existential companion of the everyday life of humanity's progression and regression, starting with the early food gathering work till the present high-tech operational culture. In contrast, tangent to time, the labor value is ossified in the final product. It is the temporality stupid, the driving force moving the visible collective value of labor, the primitive *accumulation*, towards an abstract and invisible entity as production activities are transformed from artisanal to mechanical reproducibility. In this mutation, the excess produced by labor, the Marxian exchange value, is, according to Derrida, "the birth of Capital. Of mysticism and the secret."[41] The mystics is indeed the fetishism of commodities which has nothing to do with the use-value, Derrida reminds us. I am not in the position to elaborate on the Marxian theory of labor value; however, I wish to share with the reader the two approaches to labor implied in the architectural theorization of the nineteenth century. On the one hand, we have the views advocated by John Ruskin of the Arts and Crafts movement, and the Semper of the four elements of architecture.

In the *Seven Lamps of Architecture* (1849), Ruskin inks the subject of labor in architecture page after page. However, his moral and Christian ethos was theoretical obstacles to formulating an advanced position on the issue. Welcoming *sacrifice*, Ruskin saw in the increase of labor the genesis of beauty in architecture. He was less concerned with the toil of making but the labor of hand transforming the building into architecture. And yet considering his sympathy with Gothic forms, Ruskin might have been aware of the sacrifice involved in extinguishing the labor performed in the guild systems tidy to the order of the time, commodification.[42] This and numerous instances evident in Ruskin's text, we should say that his regressive ethos made Semper sound materialist to Ruskin's contemporaries. I will go further and posit that one reason for the topicality of Semper in our digital age relates to the fact that instead of preserving a few aspects of simpler past eras, the German architect resigned to raise against the "creative destructiveness" of rising capitalism.[43]

Semper's praise of gas lighting paralleled Marx, who, according to Jameson, had personal delight "in new technologies and scientific discoveries," for one thing, to measure their impact on his theory of labor value, but also "evade the ever-present temptation of nostalgia for a simpler past and for retreat into human pre-capitalist modes of production,"[44] as was the case with Ruskin and other advocates of guild-based craftsmanship. Theirs was to resist submitting to a functional object (the table Marx discusses in the first volume of *Capital*) that would "stand on its head" upon entering the circuit of exchanges.[45] I will come back to the implied *theatricality*. For now, I want to say that most Ruskinians of the time wanted to see and emulate an object merely along the body's life and as part of existential and phenomenological experience, reconceiving the "work into aesthetic activity." This much is evident from the distinction Ruskin made between building and architecture. Whereas the former is expected to stand firm even using machine tools, architecture must bestow building "characters venerable or beautiful, but otherwise unnecessary."[46] Here excess, ornament, in particular, is conditioned by the "abstract beauty of its form" and the "sense of human labor and care spent upon it." Ruskin was not only nostalgic for the pre-industrial state of labor and productivity, but he also avoided accepting that by the advent of mechanical reproducibility, a different state of seeing and making had emerged that was not technical but part of the aesthetic of commodity form. While Ruskin would have agreed with Marx that the machine does not free the worker from work, it deprives the work itself of all content, as discussed extensively by Hannah Arendt.[47] And yet, Ruskin's uncritical emulation of "human content" was another dimension of his yearning for Christian Gothic architecture and the community of hands elevating the cathedral's stones into a work of architecture. Focusing dogmatically on "making," Ruskin failed to see the Gothic cathedrals in the context of the city, something Bramante had already recognized. For this advocate of "no style," the Gothic "cannot be treated as an ideological problem."[48] Even William Morris's ideological confusion was to consider ornament synonymous with freedom from manual labor, whereas, for Loos, it was a parasitic addition to the toil of the worker already dragged to a mechanized division of labor. "The working hand becomes dangerous when, through its song in the ornament, it supports the worker's demand for self-determination, the demand of the moment. It is necessary that the working hand fads," writes Arantes Pedro Fiori.[49]

The ideological canvas spread by digital rehabilitation of ornament is overwhelming enough to force Rem Koolhaas to say, "I do not see any utopian model … So what is left to the architect but to design beautiful ornaments? Period."[50] Were not similar statements uttered to sell the postmodern kitsch? The issue of labor and ornament has attained more complexity in the post-colonial nations raising questions like this; should the traces of construction left on the concrete surfaces of the post-independent Indian architecture be considered ornament or the scarcity of labor?[51] The fact is that by the late nineteenth century, the inclusion of concrete in design cast a calculative light on time and labor consumed by brick masons, not to mention their political power as organized labor, at least in England.[52] The politicization of construction sites has attained a new momentum by the globalization of know-how and its exportation to "developing countries," essential for the capitalistic progress primarily focused on cheap labor availability. Construction workers in developing countries are thus pressured to lose their traditional skills because of the national modernization of the building industry and the importation of materials, techniques, and skills required to build digitally reproduced architecture. Should we say that the plantation of various building types designed by western architects in oil-rich countries is symptomatic of showcasing the capitalistic image of global modernization? Interestingly, the constant introduction of new digital programming has alienated architects from design and construction sites. Star architects of my generation rely mainly on the young graduates from Ivy League universities, at least in the States.

To further elucidate the differences between Ruskin and Semper, I would like to reiterate Benjamin's references to Semper mentioned earlier. To follow Benjamin, the implied excess in the "festive occasion of life" was part of mass internalization and consumption of the aestheticization induced by mechanical reproducibility. I will extend the affiliation of Semper's theorization of architecture with the onslaught of commodity form to include the architect's notion of *Stoffwechsel, which means* "material transformation," which gained popularity among German materialist thinkers. However, for Semper, it signified the material transformation of artistic motifs from one state of productivity to another.[53] How decorative elements of Egyptian women's hair were used in the column's capital; for one, among many other examples, Semper elaborates on the textiles section of *Der Stil*. Here lies the productive autonomy Semper charged to motifs regardless of their technical and moral origins. More specifically, it is essential to underline the dynamic (movement) implied in *Stoffwechsel*, denoting biological and "metabolic processes." For Semper, artistic forms "undergo changes of material but carry forward vestiges or residues of their earlier material styles in later forms..."[54] Under the auspices of technological innovations, a similar transaction also takes place between two temporalities of labor, one preserving while the other transforming the existing forms. Marx wrote, "for not only does labor power produce a new value, on the one hand, it also resurrects older stored or dead value in the 'means' as well as the 'raw materials on the other.'"[55]

So far, I have mapped the subject of labor in the dialectical understanding of the similarities and differences between the state of architectural debate in the late nineteenth century and the present. In particular, I have insisted that the duality between construction and ornament is central to architecture. In addition to these two, there is a third factor suggested in Semper's concept of theatricality. To dispense with both sides of the debate stressing the primacy of ornament or construction, architecture is better off with Semper. The excess implied in Semper's tectonic of theatricality can be grasped in comparison to the body of a ballerina who jumps up and stands firm and figural. As such, theatricality differs from pretentious appearances of dressed-up figures performing in a carnival.[56] This comparison is helpful considering the *objectile* nature of digitally reproduced architecture that, according to Bernard Cache, "falls away from the supporting structure and hangs like an oversized piece of clothing."[57] And yet, we should not forget that the duality between construction and ornament discloses the ideology of labor in architectural theories of the time, which must be reapproached in place of critical importance of the frame-skin tectonics for the formation of modern architecture. The significance of tectonics and detailing rests in demonstrating the residues of the useful labor resisting its extinction in commodity form, the objectile character of parametric architecture. Knowingly that the traces of production are smothered in the process of digital reproducibility, what should concern us is the *appearance* of the work, that additional layer of labor that transforms the material into materiality, from rope to knot, to use a Semperian analog. Like a well-thought detailing, the knot adds a new value to the rope without annihilating the labor invested. In so doing, the knot discloses the dual temporalities pertinent to the production of the rope and its reproduction into the new form. This dialectical transformation, paradoxically, "renders the past of production immensely more present at the same time that it is invisible, having been effaced in the process by 'extinguishing,'" to recall Jameson again.[58]

Ruskin could have agreed with the above comparison at the expense of further insisting on nostalgic yearning for the stoned appearance of Gothic cathedrals. On the other hand, Semper was optimistic about the transformation induced by modern techniques as far as he could hold on to the tectonics of the core-form and the art-form. Whereas the value of labor necessarily extinguishes in the process of production, it remains as such even in more advanced stages of civilization. This amounts to the currency of these two nineteenth-century architects today. Most architects theorizing digital architecture either dwell on Semper or Ruskin. In addition to Cache, we are reminded of Lars Spuybroek and his excavation into the digital nature of Gothic. Looking at Gothic cathedrals from Ruskin's eyes, we might see the "savageness" of Gothic because it lets the worker, the stonemason, decide what to do at the cost of making correctable mistakes in the case with digitally programmed machines. Accordingly, Ruskin understood how force and formwork in Gothic contradicted the "proportional variation" of Renaissance architecture and the Semperian tectonic of theatricality.[59]

A Laborious Ending!

I want to argue that architecture's difference from other commodities further complicates the invisibility of labor. Contrary to most commodities, architecture is a static object and cannot be circulated in the worldwide marketing space of capitalism except in image form. Architecture, by necessity, is anchored to place not just to prove its regional dimension but to demonstrate the space-place complexity beyond the advocates of both sides of the divide. Still, being rooted in a place and unable to float in any space except virtual networks, architecture has established its essentiality for the spatial environment of the everyday-life, extending its active presence in the city's domain. And yet, if it is not appropriated as a visual object, architecture's primary experience unfolds in a distracted state as its internal space collides with a particular purpose. Still, many factors, formal, tactile, light, and shadow, play a decisive role in the internal organization of a building detectible in the planimetric and sectional drawings.

In haste and besides what I have said in previous pages, under the auspices of the metaphysics of mimesis, most planimetric organizations associated with the culture of Humanism (except the Baroque) were coordinated with the front and back, left and right dualities of the body. Thanks to the structural frame system and the concept of free-plan and Raum-plan, the classical concept of plan was deconstructed in many ways. The circulatory system in Le Corbusier's work is experienced in analogy to the filmic camera. In Loos's work, the body moves around, up, and down, and similar to Le Corbusier's work, the spatial experience takes place in diachronic rather than synchronic correspondence to the body's position. In the case of Mies, to limit the comparison to three architects peppering previous pages, the movement experienced in many variations of open-plan is suspended, leaving the body with self-existential and sensuousness appreciation of its solitude wrapped in a curtain and the absence of any material distraction prolific in Loos and occasionally taken into consideration in Le Corbusier's architecture, Maison Jaoul for instance. This aspect of modern architecture is better understood along with Reinhart Koselleck's historiographic conjunction between "space of experience" and "horizon of expectation," foreshadowing historical time,[60] the uniqueness of the zeitgeist of modernity. Useful Koselleck's conceptual pair for historiography, nevertheless, with Theodor Adorno's formulation of "culture industry" and its dissemination beyond the mental map of the place and national identity, the contemporaneity of horizon of expectation surpasses the spatial organization of architecture and is reconceived either about classical canons or in consideration to the dichotomous rapport between modernity and tradition. This unfolding, I posit, is another dimension of the present crisis of architectural praxis.

And yet, the dialogical rapport between space and place informing the interiority of architecture further obscures the tangibility of labor beyond the dual nature of labor evident in every commodity. This observation foreshadows one of the responsibilities of the architect; how to bring forth the invisible labor in the final work. For example, in Maison Jaoul, the architect departs from the Purist forms of Villa Savoye prone to the tactile sensibilities of load-bearing crude brick walls with unstruck mortar joints, exposed concrete

Figure 4.1 Zaha Hadid, Heydar Aliyev Cultural Center, Baku, 2014.

Source: Image courtesy of Zaha Hadid Architects.

beams, and Catalan tiles, which, according to Frampton, were "an affront to those architects who had been nurtured on the myth that modern architecture was necessarily machinist and planar and above all sustained by an elegant and articulate structural frame."[61] Here, Frampton expresses a Benjaminian passion for unearthing the past, contrasting the vernacular culture of building in modern conditions with the straitjacket modernism tailored by the technification of architecture.

To further elucidate my point, we should make a brief comparative analysis between Zaha Hadid's Heydar Aliyev Cultural Center (Figure 4.1), Baku (2013), and Jørn Utzon's Opera House (Figure 4.2), Sydney (1973). Using the most advanced computational system, the former work demonstrates an undulating and soft-looking skin supported by a concrete structure combined with a space frame system. A composite construction system compromises the building's frame structure wherein tectonics of skin and bone gives way to a rising and falling structural envelope. With this gesture, "the building blurs the conventional differentiation between architectural object and urban landscape, building envelope and urban plaza, figure, and ground, interior, and exterior."[62] The project's delicate tectonic grounding of the earth-work and the frame-work (to use Semperian terminology), on the other hand, is a reminder of Utzon's Opera House, Sydney, with this difference: Utzon's original shell, the roof-work, had to be edited and replaced by a semi-ribbed frame and shell system. Frampton writes, "Utzon's Sydney proves the point that a tectonic

Figure 4.2 Jørn Utzon, Sydney Opera House (interior) Sydney, Australia, 1973.
Source: Photograph by the author.

concept and a structurally rational work may not necessarily coin-
cide; a disfunction that recalls Damisch's critique of Viollet-le-Duc
that there is always some inescapable gap between the constructional
means and the architectonic result."[63] This tectonic consideration
necessitated a construction system combining steel, wood, and concrete structural elements. Instead of smothering material and structural differences, Utzon highlighted materiality, charging the work
with sophisticated joint-work and detailing evident in the interior
and exterior surfaces of the building. It is a Semperian call, "deliberately stressing how the parts are connected and interlaced towards a
common end, all the more eloquently as coordinated and unified."[64]
Still, and in contradistinction to most parametric work, what stands

out in Utzon's work is the tectonic articulation of roofing and terrace making. By contrast, nothing demonstrates the atectonic quality of Hadid's Heydar Aliyev project better than the smooth undulating interior and exterior surfaces. Similar to the overwhelming presence of the commodity-form image, the surface in Hadid's project is seemingly conceived independent of its structure. In the interior of Heydar Aliyev, detailing is dispensed at the expense of a white hollow, as if wrapping the spectator's body.

To make the above observation theoretically more conclusive, it is useful to recall Benjamin in "The Author as Producer," written in the early 1930s, unpublished during his lifetime.[65] Even though his essay is focused on literature, it makes sense to conclude this chapter with his two-tire analysis of the work's position within the political economy of the time. Benjamin was convinced that the content of a literary work enjoys a certain degree of autonomy despite the economic structure of the publication processes, that is, some total of the prevailing system of labor and technique. Accordingly, instead of asking how architecture should respond to the quantifiable dimension of "construction," we should ask how the work resists immersing into the ideological fabric of capitalism, the prevailing spectacle, and the aestheticization of the dichotomy between the core-form and the art-form, to stay with Semper. To follow Benjamin, architects are producers in the double sense of the term; the choices they make in detailing and the perceived connectivity among various construction parts are not entirely separate from the art-form, the image in the architect's mind. Dialectically, a critical awareness of the prevailing aesthetics should force the architect to think of the core-form, not in terms of the "realism" of the available labor and techniques. Addressing a gathering of antifascist intellectuals, Benjamin proclaimed that "the tendency of a literal work can be politically correct only if it is also literally correct."[66] And Jameson writes, "the political sin of what we call modernism is not technical innovation and experimentation, as in the realism debates; it is aestheticism as such, the consumption of beauty."[67] This is also evident in Benjamin's comparison of John Heartfield's photomontages with Renger Patzsch's photographs. Whereas the former used the technique of photomontage to reveal the political nature of the German Nazi regime, the latter used photographic images to showcase the beauty that technology can offer. Apropos, the criticism of parametric architecture launched throughout this volume is not technological but the architect's ideological drive for the theatricalization of the work. I make this proposition unabashedly in recollection of the work of Russian Constructivism in contradistinction to the Stalinist dogmas that forced architecture to mirror the state apparatus, the "base" that had not changed. What was changed was the Constructivist attempt to underline the collectivist dimension of architecture.[68]

Now, what should we learn from the historicity of the historical avant-garde today? For one thing, contrary to the contemporary situation that the spectacle of capitalism is experienced overwhelmingly, almost to the point of emulating it as natural, during the 1920s, there was still space for progressive artists and architects to think and implement techniques to critique the rising capitalism. In stating the dialectical rapport between the Real and subjectivity, Marx suggested that humanity asks questions that can solve them. Interestingly, Le Corbusier wrote that the solution to a problem is implied in the question if stated correctly. In the last chapter of *Towards an Architecture* (1924), he wittingly claimed that "revolution" can be avoided if the choice were between "architecture or revolution?" In retrospect, the architect's decision to side with the art of building was a constructive choice; from his architecture of *purism* to the brutalism attributed to his later work, Le Corbusier tried to recode the *interiority* of architecture as capitalism moved from solving one set of problems, caused by its internal contradictions to another set. Along this battle line, criticism cannot be succinct if it is not directed against architects and academic institutions when, under the name of *reform* and the technocratic idea of *transdisciplinarity*, most decisions tend to negate disciplines that are not profitable enough, cutting history/theory courses, to suit the curriculum's demands for the technification of architecture. To formulate a critical account of architecture and labor, we need fresh air!

Notes

1 "Back to Work," was published in Aaron Cayer, Peggy Deamer, Sben Korsh, Eric Peterson, and Manual Shvartzberg, *Asymmetric Labors: The Economy of Architecture in Theory and Practice* (New York: The Architecture Lobby, 2016). I want take this opportunity to thank Deamer for inviting to be part of the project.

2 Girogio Agamben, *Stanzas: World and Phantasm in Western Culture* (Minneapolis: University of Minneapolis Press, 1993), 37.

3 Theodor Adorno, "Music and Technology," in *Sound of Figures* (Stanford: Stanford University Press, 1994).

4 Alois Riegl, "Mood as the Content of Modern Art," *Grey Room* (Summer 2020): 26–37. Alois Riegl's article was published in 1899, and this first time English edition was translated by Lucia Allais and Andrei Pop. Adolf Loos's description of the vernacular milieu also recalls Walter Benjamin's

theorization of aura in the famous essay "The Work of Art in the Age of Technological Reproducibility," in *Walter Benjamin: Selected Writings, Volume 4, 1938-1940* (Cambridge: Harvard University Press, 2003), 251–283, footnote 11, p. 272 in particular.

5 Joseph Rykwert, *The Necessity of Artifice* (New York: Rizzoli International Publications Inc., 1982), 71.

6 Hubert Danisch, Noah's Ark: Essays on Architecture (Cambridge: The MIT Press, 2016), 40.

7 Hal Foster, *Design and Crime* (London: Verso Books, 2002), 15.

8 Joseph Rykwert, *The Necessity of Artifice*, 1982, 71.

9 These are part of Theodor Adorno's criticism of Martin Heidegger. See Adorno, *The Jargon of Authenticity* (Evanston: Northwestern University Press, 1973), 108.

10 See Fredric Jameson's reading of Walter Benjamin in The *Benjamin's Files* (London: Verso Books, 2020), 76.

11 See S. Zizek's reading of Gill Deleuz. Slavoj Zizek, *Organs Without Bodies: On Deleuz and Consequences* (London: Routledge, 2012), 12.

12 Hubert Damisch, 2016, 227.

13 Fredric Jameson, *The Benjamin Files*, 2020, 7.

14 Theodor Adorno, *Kierkegaard, Construction of Aesthetic* (Minneapolis: University of Minneapolis Press, 1989), 47. Quoted also in Fredric Jameson, *The Benjamin's Files* (London: Verso Books, 2020), 44.

15 Fredric Jameson, The *Benjamin's Files*, 2020, 93.

16 Fredric J. Schwartz, "Peter Weiss: Art and the Historiography of Resistance," *Journal of Art History* (2012), 81:2, 70.

17 Here and as mentioned above, I am benefitting Fredric Jameson's insightful reading of "gambling." See Jameson, *The Benjamin's Files*, 2020, 93–94.

18 Gottfried Semper, *The Four Elements of Architecture and Other Writings*, Harry F. Mallgrave and Wolfgang Herrmann, trans. (Cambridge: Cambridge University Press, 1989), 215–263.

19 Harry-Francis Mallgrave, *RES* (Autumn 1983): 25.

20 Reinhart Koselleck, *Futures Past: On the Semantics of Historical Time* (New York: Columbia University Press, 1979), 260.

21 Joseph Rykwert, *RES* (Autumn 1983): 7.

22 Jean Baudrillard, The Mirror of Production (St. Louis: Telos Press, 1975), 22.

23 Walter Benjamin, *The Arcades Project* (Cambridge: Harvard University Press, 1999), 460.

24 Susan Buck-Morss discusses how "technology affected the social imaginary" in "Aesthetic and Anaesthetics: Walter Benjamin's Artwork Essay Reconsidered," *October* 62 (Fall 1992); 30.

25 Walter Benjamin, *The Arcades Project* (Cambridge: Harvard University Press, 1999), 569–570. Semper's quotation is from his *Wissenschaft: Industrie und Kunst*, 1852.

26 Benjamin H.D. Buchloh, "Ilse Bing: A Frankfurt School Photographer in Paris and New York," *October* 173 (Summer 2020): 176–206.

27 Christian Lodder, *Russian Constructivism* (New Haven, CT: Yale University Press, 1983), 38.

28 Peter Weiss quoted in Fredric Jameson (2020), 158.

29 Walter Benjamin, "The Work of Art in the Age of Mechanical Reproduction," in *Illuminations* (New York: Schocken, 1969), 223.

30 Fredric Jameson, "Architecture and the Critique of Ideology," in *The Ideologies of Theory* (London: Verso Books, 2008), 344–371.

31 Arantes Pedro Fiori, *The Forms of Rent: Architecture and Labor in the Digital Age* (Minneapolis: The University of Minnesota Press, 2019), 213.

32 Fredric Jameson, 2008, 465–466.

33 Hal Foster, *What Comes After Farce* (London: Verso Books, 2020), 91.

34 Fredrick Jameson, The *Benjamin's Files* (London: Verso Books, 2020), 307.

35 Arantes Pedro Fiori, *The Rent of Form: Architecture and Labor in the Digital Age* (Minneapolis: University of Minnesota, 206), 7.

36 Fredric Jameson, "Time and the Concept of Modernity," in Cynthia C. Davidson ed., *Anytime* (Cambridge: The MIT Press, 1999), 208–2017.

37 Fredric Jameson, 1999.

38 Alvaro Siza, *Imagining the Evident* (Lisboa: Monade, 2021), 41.

39 Wilfried Wang, "Site-Specificity, Skilled Labor and Culture: Architectural Principles in the Age of Climate Change," in K. Cavarana, Briton and Robert McCarter, ed. *Modern Architecture and the Lifeworld: Essays in Honor of Kenneth Frampton* (London: Thames & Hudson, 2022), 56.

40 Walter Benjamin, *The Origin of German Tragic Drama* (London: Verso Books, 1977), 235.

41 Jacque Derrida, *Specters of Marx* (London: Routledge, 1994), 147.

42 Fredric Jameson, *Representing Capital*, 2011, 59.

43 Fredric Jameson, *Representing Capital*, 2011, 89.

44 Fredric Jameson, *Representing Capital: A Reading of Volume One* (London: Verso Books, 2011), 8.

45 Girogio Agamben, *Stanzas*, 1993, 37

46 John Ruskin, *The Seven Lamps of Architecture* (New York: Farrar, Straus and Giroux, 1981), 16.

47 Hannah Arendt, *The Human Condition* (Chicago: Unversity of Chicago Press, 1958). And Kenneth Frampton's appraisal of her work in "The Status of Man and the Status of His Object," Guest Edited by Kenneth Frampton, *Modern Architecture and the Critical Present* (London: Architectural Design, 1982), 20–27, special issue of *Architectural Design Profile* on the occasion of the Publication of Frampton's *Critical History*, 1980.

48 Pier Paolo Tamburelli, *On Bramante* (Cambridge: The MIT Press, 2022), 16–19.

49 Arantes Pedro Fiori, *The Forms of Rent*, 2019, 48.

50 Arantes Pedro Fiori, 2019, 52.

51 Martino Stierli, "The Politics of Concrte," in V. Prakash, M. Casciato, and D.E. Coslett, ed. *Rethinking Global Modernism: Architectural Historiography and the Postcolonial* (London: Routledge, 2022), 278–279.

52 Arantes Pedro Fiori, *The Forms of Rent*, 2019, 148.

53 See Harry-Francis Mallgrave, *Gottfried Semper: Architect of the Nineteenth Century* (New Haven: Yale University Press, 1996), 284.

54 Harry-Francis Mallgrave, 1996, 284.

55 Karl Marx wrote; "The old form of the use-value disappears, but it is taken up again in a new form of use-value." Quoted in Fredric Jameson, *Representing Capital: A Reading of Volume One* (London: Verso Books, 2011), 99.

56 On this subject, see Gevork Hartoonian, "The Fabric of Fabrication," *Textile*, vol. 4, no 3 (2006): 270–291.

57 Bernard Cahe, *Earth Moves: The Furnishing of Territories* (Cambridge: MIT Press, 1995), 70.

58 Fredric Jameson, *Representing Capital* (2011), 102.

59 Lars Spuybroek, *The Sympathy of Things: Ruskin and the Ecology of Design* (London: Routledge, 2016), 6.

60 Reinhart Koselleck, *Futures Past*, 1979. I am also thinking of the notion of historicity in Walter Benjamin's take on History. Fredric Jameson, *The Benjamin Files*, 2019, 227–228.

61 Kenneth Frampton, *Le Corbusier* (London: Thames & Hudson, 2001), 146.

62 See http://www.archdaily.com/448774/heydar-aliyev-center-zaha-hadid-architects/ accessed, Nov. 7, 2014, 11 am.

63 Kenneth Frampton, *Studies in Tectonic Culture: The Poetics of Construction in Nineteenth and Twentieth Century Architecture* (Cambridge: The MIT Press, 2001), 273.

64 Gottfried Semper, *Style in Technical and Tectonic Arts; or Practical Aesthetics* (Santa Monica: The Getty Center, 2004), 154.

65 Walter Benjamin, "The Author as Producer," in *Walter Benjamin: Selected Writings, vol. 2, 1927–1934* (Cambridge: Harvard University Press, 1999), 768–782. I am also benefiting from Fredric Jameson's take on Benjamin's essay. Jameson, *The Benjamin Files*, 2020, 208–218.

66 Walter Benjamin, "*The Author as Producer*," 1999, 769.

67 Fredric Jameson, *The Benjamin Files*, 2020, 213.

68 Jean-Louis Cohen with Ross Wolfe: "Architecture and Revolution," *The Brooklyn* Rail (November 2020).

Afterword

The four essays collected in this volume present a particular position on architecture's autonomy. Throughout Modernity, architecture had to modify its disciplinarity according to innovative ideas, techniques, and materials that were not available during pre-modern architectural praxis. Most contemporary reflections on architecture autonomy disclose revisionistic readings of Le Corbusier's Five Points of Architecture, developed in the 1920s in analogy to the classical traditions of architecture and industrial products such as silos and cars. A brief survey of architectural tendencies developed within the temporal gamut of the 1960s to the late 1980s is convincing to say that "autonomy" was considered a conceptual tool to reenergize architecture. To this end, it was deemed necessary to conceive architecture as an *object* to be recharged with new semantics borrowed from old and new theories, including semiotics, structuralism, post-structuralism, and the Derridean deconstruction theory. Bernard Tschumi, for one, wrote that the 1970s drive for autonomy was sought against those who would propagate architecture to represent cultural and regional identities (phenomenology?). According to him, formalism and regionalism dismiss "the multiplicity of heterogeneous discourses, the constant interaction between movement, sensual experience, and conceptual acrobatics that refute the parallel with the visual arts."[1] Tschumi's statement speaks for architecture's tendency to internalize ideas and concepts that are extraneous to the discipline. Accordingly, a crack occurred between history and theory, turning the balance in favor of Theory.

Elsewhere, I have extensively discussed the historicity of autonomy.[2] Here, I intend to sharpen the complex issue of critical discourse and its rapport with the given historical conditions. Critiquing the formalism of the 1960s, Stanford Anderson advocated a semi-autonomous position, suggesting that Le Corbusier's Five Points is open to "general propositions about space, light, and environmental organization, ..."[3] Mention should also be made of Kenneth Frampton's discourse on "critical regionalism" and typological and morphological investigations initiated by the Italian *Tendenza group*.[4] The history theme underpins these theorizations, suggesting that autonomy should not be taken literally, even in its most formalistic interpretation. Accordingly, even in its formalist moments, architecture, in one way or another, is part of its temporality, be it techno-economics (the early modernism) or historicist (postmodernism of the late 1970s), and the spectacle informing contemporary architecture. This development, I posit, has paved the way for the realization of the third state of objectivity, much in conformity with what Walter Benjamin coined the "exhibition value" of the work. Thus, the building art has come full circle: from the Bauhaus solidification of the late nineteenth-century push to transform ornament into *object*; to the realization of the Modernist notion of objectivity; and finally, the transformation from Modernism to the current situation where architecture has become ornament par excellence. In this permutation, we witness the proliferation of various strategies, each justifying architecture's adaptation to capitalism's aesthetic and technological apparatuses.

The third stage of objectivity attests to architecture's loss of agency for the collective, the social housing of the 1920s or the 1950s esteem for civic architecture and monumentality. The paradox in this turn of events is that architecture today has become a significant component of the present culture of spectacle and its most popular advocate. In this metamorphosis, architecture has lost its Modernist vanguard mission that, interestingly enough, had to do with a sense of *autonomy* sustained by the desire to distance architecture from a culture that was not yet modernized. Instead, architecture has slowly but surely turned into an aestheticized object. If this is a plausible assessment of architecture's contemporaneity, then the four essays of this book offer the thematic of critical practice. I want to highlight this claim because of notable similarities between what I argued in 2014 (see footnote 2 below) and Hal Foster's recent observation that "art, to be critical, must be immanent to the structures of its world,"[5] and spectacle in particular. How Gottfried Semper comes into this picture?

To assess architecture's rapport with the Real, I would like to draw the reader's attention to the work of a few American artists of the late 1950s, Andy Warhol, Cales Oldenburg, and Roy Lichtenstein, each using banal consumer goods and populist figures of the time as the subject matter of painting.[6] If at one point their work was viewed in the shadow of the historical avant-garde, today, the dialectical nature of their work is part of a direct encounter with the culture industry. We could extend this judgment to postmodern architecture and disclose the ongoing tension between autonomy and objectivity since architecture's inevitable entry into the process of mechanical reproducibility, the Adornoesque "culture industry." Dressed up in the garment of pre-modern languages, postmodern architecture paved the way for digitally reproduced architecture. In both instances, the tectonic potentialities of the Corbusian Dom-ino frame, the tension between skin and bone, were defused, promoting a discourse of autonomy primarily focused on the *surface* now in analogy to the network of media technologies. Not only should the suggested tension be revisited today, but the political should be sought in the discourse of tectonic, highlighting the essentiality of material, labor, and techniques for architecture at a moment when the nihilism of technology is paramount in every aspect of the present everyday life.

As discussed throughout this volume, Semper's tectonic theory is of interest today, not only because the tectonics dispensed with the traditions of mimesis are at the dawn of modernization but also because Semper was not hesitant to submit architecture to the vicissitudes of industrial techniques. Taking clues from the four industries, tectonics was a radical project to disband the classical notion of objectivity, if only to revisit aspects of it in the light of the tectonic split between the art-form and the core-form. Apropos, Semper's theorization of architecture anticipated the two interrelated elements of modernism, the tension between skin and structure and the importance of image for the modernist aesthetic experience. Accordingly, architecture attained visibility in the prevailing realm of culture without dispensing with the interiority of architecture, that is, what is architectural in construction. Internalizing the nihilism of technology, tectonics suspends this process of internalization by the very fact that construction is *fabrication* and anathema to the spectacle. In analogy to Benjamin's "exhibition value," stated at the end of his famous work of art essay, the particular in theatrical tectonics is its capacity to internalize the nihilism of technology to demonstrate the thriving task of architecture *for-itself*, autonomy proper. It also offers a dialectical play between the technical and mental to the point that technique becomes cognitive, and "intelligence becomes technique and labor."[7] I propose this was what Mies van der Rohe meant when he declared, "Whenever technology reaches its real fulfillment, it transcends into architecture."[8] The diffusion of opposites as such plots autonomy in the matrix of disciplinary history of architecture and techniques external to that history. Tectonics, as discussed in this book, opens a horizon where the present euphoria for the spectacle meets aspects of making that are of vital interest to the longevity of capitalism. A case in point is Mies's later work; a module called the 50x50 House (1950) that was reproduced for other building types, from the Bacardi office building (1957) to the Berlin National Gallery (1968). Internalizing "seriality," the fundamental index of modern society that, according to Foster,[9] runs through various artwork of the 1960s, Mies turned the nihilism of technology into tectonics wherein the classical rapport between the column and beam was radically deconstructed at the expense of *surface* not only in terms of the modernist and postmodernist free-facade but also the morphing surfaces of digitally reproduced architecture. Perhaps that is why Mies hesitated to use the term "architecture" instead of *Baukunst*, the art of building.

Notes

1 Bernard Tschumi, "Architecture and Limits III," *Artforum*, September (1981): 40.
2 Gevork Hartoonian, "Capitalism and the Politics of Autonomy," in Nadir Lahiji, ed. *Architecture Against the Post-Political: Essays in Reclaiming the Critical Project* (London: Routledge, 2014), 69–83.
3 Stanford Anderson, "Quasi-Autonomy in Architecture: The Search for an 'In-Between'," *Perspecta*, vol. 33 (2002): 30–37.
4 See Pier Vittorio Aureli, *The Project of Autonomy: Politics and Architecture Within and Against Capitalism* (Princeton: Princeton University Press, 2012).
5 Hal Foster, "Antinomies," *Artforum*, September (2022) https://www.artforum.com/print/202207/antinomies-88911, viewed Sunday, September 4, 2022. Also, see Foster, "Seriality, Sociability, Silence," *Artforum*, December 2020.
6 The following observation was part of my reaction to two exhibitions at the Metropolitan Museum of Art, New York City, 2012, and the National Gallery of Art, Washington D. C., 2012.
7 Jacques Ranciere, Aesthetics and its Discontent (Cambridge: Polity Press, 2009), 23.
8 Mies van der Rohe, "Technology and Architecture," in Ulrich Conrads, ed. *Programs and Manifestoes on 20th-Century Architecture* (Cambridge: The MIT Press, 1975), 154.
9 The idea was promoted by Jean-Paul Sartre in 1960, and Hal Foster how Andy Warhol and Barbara Kruger turned it into action. Foster, "Seriality, Sociability, Silence," *Artforum*, 2020.

Index

Printed in the United States
by Baker & Taylor Publisher Services